The Railways, the Market and the Government

The Railways, the Market and the Government

WITH CONTRIBUTIONS FROM
JOHN HIBBS
OLIVER KNIPPING
RICO MERKERT
CHRIS NASH
RANA ROY
DAVID E. TYRRALL
RICHARD WELLINGS

The Institute of Economic Affairs

First published in Great Britain in 2006 by
The Institute of Economic Affairs
2 Lord North Street
Westminster
London SW1P 3LB
in association with Profile Books Ltd

The mission of the Institute of Economic Affairs is to improve public understanding of the fundamental institutions of a free society, with particular reference to the role of markets in solving economic and social problems.

Copyright © The Institute of Economic Affairs 2006

The moral right of the authors has been asserted.

All rights reserved. Without limiting the rights under copyright reserved above, no part of this publication may be reproduced, stored or introduced into a retrieval system, or transmitted, in any form or by any means (electronic, mechanical, photocopying, recording or otherwise), without the prior written permission of both the copyright owner and the publisher of this book.

A CIP catalogue record for this book is available from the British Library.

ISBN-10: 0 255 36567 5
ISBN-13: 978 0 255 36567 3

Many IEA publications are translated into languages other than English or are reprinted. Permission to translate or to reprint should be sought from the Director General at the address above.

Typeset in Stone by MacGuru Ltd
info@macguru.org.uk

Printed and bound in Great Britain by Hobbs the Printers

CONTENTS

The authors	9
Foreword	13
List of tables, figures and boxes	16

PART ONE: WHO SHOULD RUN THE RAILWAYS? THE HISTORICAL CONTEXT   19

1 Railways and the power of emotion: from private to public ownership   21
John Hibbs

Feelings and reality	21
Government meddling, 1921–39	26
Monolithic management	32
What followed Beeching	41
References	44

2 Railways and the power of emotion: seeking a market solution   46
John Hibbs

A success story forgotten	46
The path to privatisation	47
Government meddling – it still goes on	52
What is so special about the railways?	58

What is the future?	61
The people problem	62
Conclusion	65
References	66

PART TWO: WHO SHOULD RUN THE RAILWAYS? AN ASSESSMENT OF RAILWAY PRIVATISATION 69

3 The restructuring of the rail system in Britain – an assessment of recent developments 71
Rico Merkert and Chris Nash

Introduction	71
The privatisation process	72
Performance since 1994	80
The rail structure review	88
Rail restructuring – success and failures	95
References	100

4 The UK railway: privatisation, efficiency and integration 105
David E. Tyrrall

Introduction	105
Privatisation: process and structure	106
The successes and failures of privatisation	109
The causes of cost failure	114
Conclusion and possible futures	120
References	125

5 Environmentalism, public choice and the railways   130
Richard Wellings
Introduction   130
Public choice theory   132
The environmental movement   135
Emissions concerns   136
Road protesters   138
The rail lobby   140
The road lobby   145
New Labour and transport policy   148
Conclusion   152
References   153

PART THREE: WHO SHOULD RUN THE RAILWAYS? THE FUTURE OF RAILWAYS AND THE MARKET ECONOMY   157

6 Railway privatisation in the UK – a laissez-faire approach to an interventionist failure   159
Oliver Knipping
Failing state railways   159
UK railways between privatisation and re-regulation   163
Towards a market for railways   169
References   176

7	**The public–private partnership and the general welfare**	179
	Rana Roy	
	Introduction: the decade of experimentation	179
	Separation, liberalisation and competition	185
	Privatisation	190
	Pricing, investment and the role of public subsidy	195
	References	208
8	**Rail in a market economy**	211
	Richard Wellings	
	Introduction	211
	Central planning and political control	212
	Transport and social cost	215
	Transport and poverty	222
	The privatised railway	224
	Distorted competition	229
	Towards free competition in transport	232
	Conclusion	237
	References	238
	About the IEA	242

THE AUTHORS

John Hibbs

John Hibbs started his career in the bus and coach industry, and later moved to British Railways' Eastern Region headquarters at Liverpool Street, where in the 1960s he was successively Traffic Survey Officer, a Costing Officer and Market Research Officer for the region. He still asks 'what's so special?' about the railway, but he retains his respect for the loyalty of managers to 'the service', which was so ill rewarded in the process of privatisation. 'Once a railwayman always a railwayman' is something he feels to this day. John Hibbs is Emeritus Professor of Transport Management at the University of Central England and has written widely on the transport industry, privatisation and road pricing. His most recent publication for the IEA was *The Dangers of Bus Re-regulation*, Occasional Paper 137.

Oliver Knipping

Oliver Knipping, PhD, is president of the Institute for Free Enterprise, Germany's free market think tank. He graduated from University College London with a PhD on railroad liberalisation in 2002 after studies in economics at Humboldt-University Berlin. Following an assignment in the German telecommunications industry on market deregulation, he is currently advising a major telecommunications provider in Croatia.

Rico Merkert

Rico Merkert is a Marie Curie Research Fellow at the Institute for Transport Studies at the University of Leeds. He previously worked in the automotive industry, at the Berlin University of Technology and at the University of Potsdam. His research work focuses on benchmarking and institutional issues in the transport sector, particularly in railways. Since 2004 he has also been a member of the national expert committee on transport policy of the German FDP.

Chris Nash

Chris Nash is Professor of Transport Economics at the Institute for Transport Studies, University of Leeds (ITS), which is one of the leading transport research groups in Great Britain, with the top (5*) rating for the quality of its research. Professor Nash leads research in the fields of rail policy and transport infrastructure charges, in which fields he has led many projects for both the British government and the European Commission. He was coordinator for the PETS, CAPRI, UNITE and IMPRINT-EUROPE projects, which sought to advance the theory and implementation of marginal-social-cost-based pricing in transport, including the quantification and valuation of transport externalities, and now leads a further European project in this area, GRACE. He has acted as expert adviser to many groups, including the High Level Group on Transport Infrastructure Charges of the EU, the Railways group of the European Conference of Ministers of Transport (ECMT), and the Transport and European Union Select Committees of the British Parliament. His current work includes advising the Office of Rail Regulation on its structure of charges review and participating in both Rail Research UK, the British Universities' rail research group, and EURNEX, the European Network of Excellence in Rail Research (for which he is a pole leader in the strategy and economics field). His publications number more than a hundred books, contributions to books and journal articles.

Rana Roy

Dr Rana Roy, FCILT, is an international consulting economist based in central London. He has worked on rail and transport-sector reform for HM Government, the European Commission and the ECMT, as well as the Railway Forum, the Community of European Railways and the International Union of Railways. Prior to setting up his own practice in 1997, Dr Roy served as Chief Economist for the European Centre for Infrastructure Studies, Economic Adviser for the UK Department of Trade and Industry, and Senior Policy Adviser for the Department of the Prime Minister and Cabinet in Australia.

David Tyrrall

David E. Tyrrall is a Senior Lecturer in Accounting and Finance at the Sir John Cass Business School, City University, London, and a fellow of the Chartered Institute of Management Accountants (CIMA) and of the Chartered Association of Certified Accountants (FCCA). He worked as an accountant and finance manager in multinational companies in the chemicals, oil and railway industries for fifteen years before becoming a university lecturer.

Richard Wellings

Dr Richard Wellings completed a PhD at the London School of Economics in 2004. His thesis examined the development of British transport policy from a public choice perspective. Subsequently, he has been working as a consultant and researcher for A & F Consulting Engineers, specialising in environmental issues. He is also writing a book about road privatisation.

FOREWORD

The building and management of Britain's railways in the mid-Victorian period was a great private enterprise success story. Though railways have never been without government interference in the UK, a relatively laissez-faire approach to their development was allowed in the first instance. When comparisons with other countries are made, it appears that this approach bore much fruit.

Unfortunately, laissez-faire did not last. The railways became a plaything of politicians. Gradually, 'coordination' and 'integration' of transport networks became something that governments thought they could achieve through bureaucratic management rather than through allowing the coordinating power of the price mechanism to operate.

The British people, as Hibbs points out in his chapters in Readings 61, have always been rather sentimental and emotional about the railways, thus making rational policy-making difficult. The railways are seen as different from other modes of transport and, therefore, special. This might be one reason why railways have mistakenly been treated and regulated as monopolies from the early days. A railway company might have a monopoly on movement by train but certainly does not have a monopoly in the market for movement as a whole. Indeed, the lack of market power of railways is indicated by the fact that they account for only about one twentieth of the total transport market.

Railway policy moved from a period of increasing regulation during the early twentieth century to outright nationalisation in the middle of that century. The management of the nationalised railways as a business was hampered by sentimental attachment to them that was out of all proportion to their declining importance in the economy. Nevertheless, in the 1980s commercial business practices came to be applied – with some satisfactory results.

This monograph traces the history of railway policy back to its earliest days. It does so because policy today, in the post-privatisation era, is still dictated by many of the same forces that dictated policy in the past. In particular, the process of privatisation in the early 1990s dictates many aspects of railway policy today.

As the chapters by Tyrrall, Wellings and Knipping make clear, at privatisation the government imposed upon the industry a structure that might never have evolved if the market had been left to itself. The splitting up of the provision of track stations and signals, the provision of rolling stock and the running of trains was a decision taken by government ministers, not business people. We would deem it nonsensical for government officials to walk into a hotel and demand that it be owned by one company, the reception and reservations be run by another company, and the beds leased from a third company. Such a division of responsibilities might be appropriate in the railway industry, but why should it be for government to decide?

Merkert and Nash argue that the basic structure of the industry at privatisation was a workable way of introducing competition, but that privatisation was marred by mistakes in implementation. Nevertheless, even many supporters of privatisation in general question whether the privatisation of the railways was a 'privatisation too far'. But why should private enterprise be any less capable of running the railways than it is the telephone, gas or bus industries? Tyrrall poses the problem that we face when analysing the success of privatisation very succinctly. The government conducted two experiments. The first was with private ownership of the railways – something that had worked before. The second was the imposition of a particular vertically disintegrated structure on the railway industry – a structure that could not easily be changed and that had never emerged before as an outcome of market processes. If the policy, taken as a whole, was deemed to be less successful than had been hoped, which experiment failed?

We cannot know the answer to this question unless we genuinely free the railways from government intervention with regard to the ownership and the corporate structure of its business. In the third part of the monograph the authors suggest various different ways of using private enterprise to best effect. Not all the authors suggest a return to the laissez-faire approach on which the success of the railways was built in the nineteenth century. All the papers in this monograph, however, contribute to improving our understanding of how railways policy in the future can be more successful than it has been in the past.

As in all IEA publications, the views expressed in this book are those of the authors and not those of the Institute (which has no corporate view), its managing trustees, Academic Advisory Council members or senior staff.

PHILIP BOOTH
Editorial and Programme Director,
Institute of Economic Affairs
Professor of Insurance and Risk Management,
Sir John Cass Business School, City University
May 2006

TABLES, FIGURES AND BOXES

Table 1	Cost of maintenance, operation and renewal of the rail network	79
Table 2	Government support to the rail industry	87
Table 3	Chronology	108

Figure 1	Rail passenger and freight volumes (1979–2002/03)	81
Figure 2	Punctuality: percentage of trains arriving on time (all operators)	82
Figure 3	Number of significant train incidents per million train kilometres	83
Figure 4	Number of broken rails per million train kilometres	84
Figure 5	Rail industry operating costs between 1989/90 and 2002/03	85
Figure 6	Rail industry capital expenditure between 1989/90 and 2002/03	86
Figure 7	Rail industry stakeholders in February 2001	107
Figure 8	UK railway passenger fatalities 1951–2004	110
Figure 9	The 1997 privatised structure: a simplified view	115
Figure 10	The proposed privatised structure: a simplified view	123
Figure 11	The layers of railway systems	171

| Box 1 | The railways ask for a square deal, 1938–9 | 33 |

The Railways, the Market and the Government

PART ONE

**WHO SHOULD RUN THE RAILWAYS?
THE HISTORICAL CONTEXT**

1 RAILWAYS AND THE POWER OF EMOTION: FROM PRIVATE TO PUBLIC OWNERSHIP
John Hibbs

Feelings and reality

Railways have a status in the public imagination today that is unrelated to their use, whether for passengers or freight. Quite apart from the closet world of the enthusiast, there is an emotional attachment to the railway, recognisable in films as far removed from each other as *Brief Encounter* and *The Titfield Thunderbolt*, and unmatched in terms of any other form of public transport on land. The adverse reaction to railway privatisation was matched by a sudden turn-around in the image of British Railways, formerly a source of music-hall jokes, so that even 'BR sandwiches' ceased to be a subject for mirth. The current fashion for reinventing the tram, in the form of 'light rapid transit', suggests that anything that runs on rails is seen to have a natural superiority in comparison with buses, and even the private car.

Where does this kind of sentimental attachment come from? As Glaister and Travers put it: '... people have an unusual and romantic attachment to railways' (Glaister and Travers, 1993: 10). How did it come about that transport policy in the British Isles has for a hundred years been biased in such a fashion that railways have been both protected and neglected at the same time? The outcome of such a distorted history has been the crisis of the present day, in which the financial future of the industry is difficult to discern. If the funds needed should come from increased fares and charges, then demand must surely fall, making such a solution impossible, yet to raise funds for the railways out of taxation must be opposed by the majority of the population for whom travel by train is of marginal importance. The problem seems to be peculiarly British, as is the phenomenon of the railway enthusiast, rarely to be found elsewhere in Europe.

In 1952 18 per cent of passenger movement in Great Britain was by train; today it is 6 per cent, the same proportion as for travel by bus and coach, which had been 42 per cent in 1952. Over the same period the increase in travel by car has been from 27 per cent to 85 per cent of all passenger movement; 71 per cent of households make regular use of cars (and 27 per cent have two or more), so the use of a car is no longer the privilege of the middle classes.

The cost of motoring, in real terms, has fallen annually for twenty years or more, and it seems destined to continue to fall. Short of point-to-point road pricing, which is a political minefield and unlikely to be introduced in a hurry, the long-distance railways must be seen to be a minority sector of the market for movement. The situation for freight movement is similar, with railways accounting for 8 per cent of tonne mileage compared with 65 per cent by road (and 27 per cent by water or pipeline).

Railways and the state

Taylor (1972) examines the conflict between interventionism and laissez-faire in the nineteenth century and quotes with approval a commentator writing in 1851 who said that 'the most important event of the last quarter of a century in English history is the establishment of Railroads'. Foster (1992) regards state ownership of utilities as a form of regulation and control. For fail-dangerous industries like the railway the need for intervention to protect innocent parties became plain from the opening of the Liverpool and Manchester Railway, in 1830, when William Huskisson, the president of the Board of Trade, was fatally injured by a locomotive, but by 1846 Peel was speaking of the activities of railway companies in creating 'a qualified monopoly'. These two themes have continued to dominate transport policy to the present day, though the distinction between them has not always been made plain.

The British railway system developed very quickly, the major trunk routes being completed in 25 years, with most secondary centres connected by 1854. While the state became involved from the start, since each new line required statutory powers,[1] the process was commercially driven and became highly expensive. But by 1859 the system was up and running, and Robbins remarks that '[The railways] were accepted by the public as a normal feature of social life' (Robbins, 1962: 33). Miller (2003) remarks that by 1867 Britain had by far the most competitive railway system of any country, but while the railway became the Victorian icon of progress there were those in the early days who were unhappy about its social consequences. The Duke of Wellington disliked railways because 'they would encourage the lower classes to move about'. Other reservations began to appear as the companies exploited economies of scale by combination, producing the impression of territorial monopoly, a phenomenon repeated in the twentieth century by the bus industry. Fear of cartelisation

---

1   In the absence of limited liability legislation the scale of railway investment required statutory authority for each line, and this also gave powers for the acquisition of land. Boundary fencing for the protection of livestock was a third factor in the parliamentary oversight of the new industry.

was encouraged by the formation in 1842 of the Railway Clearing House, although this gave the benefit of improved passenger and freight movement between companies across the system.

The second half of the nineteenth century saw the growth of a critical attitude to the railways, which remains at the heart of their political status today. Traders became suspicious that the companies were exploiting their monopoly powers, not only in their rates for carriage of goods but also by offering lower rates for imported goods. Discussing this, Barker and Savage (1974: 103) quote a statement in the *Morning Post* in 1886 saying that 'The railways exist for the public, not the public for the railways', while in the same year the *Railway Times*, speaking for the shareholders, recognised the custom 'of regarding railways not as commercial concerns, as they really are, struggling for a return on the capital invested, but as national institutions existing for the benefit of the public'.

With the passage of the Railway Regulation Act of 1840 the process began whereby the industry increasingly appeared to be a matter for political concern, the railways becoming the responsibility of the Board of Trade. Price control appeared under the Railway and Canal Traffic Act of 1854, while a similar Act of 1872 created a Railway Commission intended among other things to prevent the companies showing 'undue preference'. Safety became an increasing concern with enforcement strengthened by the Railway Regulation Act of 1889, and by the work of Her Majesty's Inspectors of Railways. Commercially the Railway & Canal Traffic Act of 1888 set up the Railway and Canal Commission, with powers to lay down maximum rates for each class of merchandise traffic. And so by the end of the century the railway industry had come to lose one central element of managerial freedom: the freedom to set its own rates and charges.

Railways and the people

By the early years of the twentieth century the train had come to be taken for granted as the natural means of travel between towns and cities, and over much of the country from villages to towns. Freight moved around the country, and served export trades such as coal as well as what in railway terms was known as merchandise traffic. Domestic coal was delivered to sidings in wagons owned by the coal merchants and the Post Office depended upon the trains. It would have been unthinkable to suggest that railways could ever become of rather minor importance, and it remained unthinkable for the rest of the century. For many people it still seems unthinkable today.

Railway companies were represented in Parliament by numerous directors, but they represented different parties and did not seem to exert the influence that might have been expected when statutory intervention was debated. But the industry was perceived to be a monopoly and therefore attracted supervision and control over and above the safety regulation. This came to a head after 1899, when the Great Central Railway opened the last main line, from Sheffield to London's Marylebone, which was quickly seen to have been a mistaken investment.

Barker and Savage (1974: 118–19) reflect upon the status of the railways and the railwaymen in the Edwardian world. They stress the increasing number of people able to travel, the increase in newspaper circulation, and 'the quite remarkable rapidity and reliability of the postal service'. 'The shareholders may have been suffering,' they continue, '... but the railway users, and the country as a whole, certainly were not.' Furthermore, they conclude, 'The equipping and maintaining of railways, both at home and overseas, was not only a cornerstone of Britain's engineering industry; it was also a significant element in the industrial life of the country as a whole.'

Government meddling, 1921–39
Pressure for change

In 1908, encouraged by Lloyd George as president of the Board of Trade, with an eye on the growing power of the unions and threats of a strike, the 'three greats' (Great Northern, Great Central and Great Eastern) promoted a Private Member's Bill that included, at the insistence of the Board of Trade, obligations 'not to diminish facilities as a whole in any district' and a guarantee that no railway jobs would go for at least three years. Unhappy at the narrow majority by which the Bill passed its second reading, the companies withdrew it, whereupon the Board of Trade set up a departmental committee. Its report in 1911 marked a turning point in railway policy, recognising that combination was inevitable 'and likely to be beneficial both to the railway companies themselves, and, if properly safeguarded, to the public also'. A strike in the same year brought the railway unions together and increased their status in the eyes of the companies and of the government. Railways were now a political issue, and a Royal Commission was set up in 1912 'to continue the quest for a magic formula which would reconcile the opposing parties' (ibid.: 117). With the outbreak of war the Commission ceased to meet, and no report was issued. By 1919 the attitude of government had changed and intervention came to the fore. In 1914 130 railway companies were taken over by the state in return for an annual sum equivalent to their net receipts for 1913. The Board of Trade was responsible for the system through a Railway Executive Committee consisting of the general managers of the ten leading companies. This experience of central control, along with the conclusions of the departmental committee, led to pressure for change. In the meantime severe logistical problems on the Western Front had been sorted out after Lloyd George had appointed Sir Eric Geddes to deal with them, and Geddes now argued for central control on a scale not to be seen again until 1947.

Central control was promoted by a Bill introduced by the government on 26 February 1918. The Bill set up a Ministry of Ways and Communications. Bagwell and Lyth (2002: 74) comment that it 'reflected Geddes's experience as transport dictator on the Western Front, rather than any understanding of long-cherished parliamentary traditions'. Neither did it suggest any understanding of the industry's traditions or of the political opposition that the Bill would meet. Clause 4 as originally designed would have given the minister power 'to own and control for the state, road and rail transport, light railways, canals and inland waterways, trams, ports and harbours, air transport and electric power' (ibid.). The general election held on 14 December 1918 meant that 174 MPs were now businessmen, but it was not the business community alone which opposed Clause 4 and led to its removal on 6 May 1919 – many local authorities also resented the loss of their municipal tramways.

As a compromise, the Act, as it finally appeared in August 1919, enabled the government to retain control of the railways for a further two years, leaving time for a new policy to be prepared. It also set up a Railway Rates Advisory Committee, which after a public inquiry made recommendations for the future. There then followed the Railways Act 1921, which became the main source of authority for government intervention and of controversy up until 1947.

What they did next

Winston Churchill is said to have commented on the future of the railways after 1919 that there was a choice between nationalisation, grouping the companies together in private ownership or leaving them alone.[2] It was the second policy which was pursued, but with some serious consequences that were to follow from another part of the 1921 Act.

The four companies[3] that were given statutory authority in 1921 were set up in 1923 and were to become the image of the railway for a generation. Of the four the Great Western continued largely unchanged both in management and esteem, imposing its standards and livery upon the smaller companies that were merged with it. The Southern was the subject of a successful makeover under its energetic general manager, Sir Herbert Walker, who not only extended electrification but created a new business out of the three railways that had been merged in 1923. Neither of the other two companies had the same success. The LMS pursued an uncertain course, not surprisingly in view of the very different traditions of its two principal components, the Midland Railway and the London & North Western. The LNER was run by three divisional general managers under Sir Ralph Wedgwood as chief general manager.

---

2 Gourvish records that Churchill, 'electioneering in Scotland in December 1918, suggested, somewhat injudiciously, that the government had definitely decided to nationalise the railways' (Gourvish, 1986: 14).

3 The Great Western, London & North Eastern, London Midland & Scottish and the Southern.

It was Part III of the Act, 'Railway Charges', that was to have more serious consequences. In place of the maximum rates and charges that had applied in principle since 1892, the Act provided for standard charges, consisting of specified rates on a tapering mileage basis, with a charge for station and service terminals, divided under eight headings for different types of traffic. The system was to be supervised by a Railway Rates Tribunal and the actual rates that came into effect on 1 January 1928 had been agreed with customers of the railways after more than 150 public sittings. It is hard to imagine a more direct intervention into commercial freedom of management than a system such as this, and yet it had an even greater impact because of the basis upon which the new rates were founded, Section 58 of the Act laying down that 'the charges to be fixed in the first instance ... shall be such as will, together with the other sources of revenue, in the opinion of the Rates Tribunal ... yield an annual net revenue ... equivalent to the aggregate net revenue in the year nineteen hundred and thirteen'.

What was the outcome?

In the 1960s the threat to railway finances came from the private car, but in the 1920s it came from commercial road motor transport. In neither case was the impact foreseen or allowed for by railway managers, civil servants or politicians. Such was the commitment to railways as a unique, essential and long-lasting monopoly supplier that the idea of an alternative supplier was unthinkable. Bagwell and Lyth (2002: 78) record 'a certain complacency on some boards of directors, most notably on the LMS board, regarding the impact of road competition', while in 1918 the Select Committee had been advised by the chairman of the Road Board in the following words, a message that seems to have been influential over subsequent years, despite growing contradictory experience: 'The special sphere of road transport will be in local distribution and as a feeder accessory to trunk systems.'

Throughout the first twenty years of the new ministry its policy leant towards the protection of the railways from competition, while the companies continued to trade under the price control set up by the 1921 Act. Road haulage developed rapidly, with long-distance services appearing in the 1930s, while bus and coach services spread even more quickly to cover the whole of the country within ten years. Middle-class car use spread as the price of new cars fell. The railway companies made no moves to close poorly performing services; instead they turned to a form of indirect cross-subsidy when after obtaining powers to operate road services in 1928 they started to acquire a substantial interest in most of the larger bus companies after 1931, competition having been limited by the Road Traffic Act 1930. A less significant interest was taken in some of the larger road freight companies after the Road & Rail Traffic Act 1933.

The 1930 Act arose out of the work of the Royal Commission on Transport set up in 1928, and specifically from the second interim report, whose recommendations were on the way to becoming law before the supporting argument appeared in the final volume. Trade union and railway pressure made the protection of the railways from road competition an objective, and this was reaffirmed by the 1933 Act, following the conclusion of the Salter Conference that 'it was not in the national interest to encourage further diversions of heavy goods traffic from the railways to the roads'.

Government intervention designed to control the railways' presumed monopoly in 1921 was a prime cause of the problems they faced in subsequent years. As Barker and Savage put it (1974: 156), 'the rigidity of the railway charges scheme inhibited railway management in competing on a commercial basis with other forms of transport', but to this must be added the impact of the depression. Government policy whose origins lay in nineteenth-century experience was unable to respond to the radical changes that might have been foreseen by the 1920s, but were not recognised even in the 1930s. Railways, it must be concluded, were accorded a special place in transport policy which was seldom questioned, and there was remarkably little debate concerning the relevant sections of the 1930 and 1933 Acts.

Conclusion

The period ended with a campaign by the four main lines for a 'Square Deal' (see Box 1). In a memorandum to the Ministry of Transport they asked for the statutory regulation of charges for merchandise to be repealed, and that the railways, 'exactly like any other forms of transport, should be permitted to decide the charges and conditions for the conveyance of merchandise which they are required to carry'. These difficulties were serious as revenues fell in difficult business times. Walker (1947: 232) records the minister's view that 'as at present advised, he is inclined to the view that in the existing circumstances there is, *prima facie*, a case for some material relaxation of existing statutory regulation, provided that due regard is had to the ultimate objective of the co-ordination of all forms of transport'. In those final words the minister expressed the way in which government policy had developed, in which the idea of coordination had become the vague but undefined objective. Before any action was taken the outbreak of war ended the argument, for the time being: though a later minister in 1943 said that 'the "Square Deal" failed to reach the root of the problem and that some more radical solution would have to be found' (ibid.: 234). Clearly the railways were not to be seen as 'just another form of transport', as the chairmen of the four main-line companies had asked that they should be.

The railway was regarded fondly and sentimentally by the public. Policy-makers were equally influenced by the supposed economic importance of rail transport, and whether by ignorance or design they failed to recognise that the transport market was becoming so much wider. 'The railways suffered from the legacy of the past in that they developed at a time when few other forms of transport were available and railway users came to rely on them for the provision of any service however uneconomic and however wasteful of the resources of the system. Hence, of course, the opposition to reform' (Dyos and Aldcroft, 1969: 312).

It is easy to dismiss public sentimentality but this did, of course, place even greater pressure on politicians who, during this age, were inclined to intervene for supposed economic and strategic reasons.

Monolithic management
The inevitable happens

That railway nationalisation would follow from the election of a Labour Party majority in the Commons in 1945 surprised nobody. Gourvish refers to 'An increasing body of opinion in all parties [which] certainly favoured a greater measure of control

Box 1 **The railways ask for a square deal, 1938–9**
Much is being said about the poor financial position of the railway industry. The real position can be stated in a few short sentences:

1 In fixing rates and conditions for carrying merchandise the Railways are bound by statutory controls and regulations which have lasted a hundred years and have grown more rigid with age.
2 No other form of goods transport is subject to such restrictions or anything comparable to them.
3 Moreover, no other form of transport has or can have such basic duties and responsibilities to the State as those which the Railways must bear at all times and more especially in times of national emergency.
4 It will be impossible for the Railways adequately to discharge those national services and duties unless they are now set free to put their house in order, and to run their business on business lines.
5 The Railways have no desire whatsoever to interfere with other transport services or with any other business.
6 They merely want the chance to put themselves right so that they may be able to set fair competition in a fair way. The main transport services should all start equal.
7 The time honoured shackles which fetter the Railways alone and well nigh strangle their goods traffic must go.
8 And they must go before it is too late.
9 A short Act of Parliament is required this session to meet a crying national need.

in the interests of both industry and the consumer' (Gourvish, 1986: 16).

But just how far the Labour leaders were committed to nationalisation remains uncertain. In a debate on nationalisation in 1929 two members asked the minister, Herbert Morrison, what was to be done to coordinate the railways and road transport. In his reply (7 November 1929) he made an interesting comment, which seems to reverberate today: 'The policy of the Government was to promote the coordination of transport undertakings but they had to recognise that the process of State interference and control of privately controlled industries often tended to give the country the worst of both worlds. It meant that the private undertakings were not free to do what they liked with their own businesses' (Hansard).

Barely three months after the 1945 Labour government had taken office the subject of transport was addressed, but the Transport Bill was to be twelve months in preparation. Bonavia records that there was little discussion of the details of the Bill, and remarks that 'One looks in vain for any estimate of the exact economic benefits to be obtained, or for any warning of possible disbenefits' (Bonavia, 1979: 18). He tells us that the government spokesmen's speeches were undistinguished, and that 'Conservative speakers tended to concentrate on irrelevancies and showed no more grasp of transport economics than Ministers and Labour backbenchers' (ibid.: 18, 21). Bagwell and Lyth comment on the Conservative Party's Industrial Charter of 1947, which they say 'accepted the need to nationalise railways, coal and the Bank of England' (Bagwell and Lyth, 2002: 126). The railway companies fought against nationalisation. The Bill received the royal assent on 6 August 1947, and the British Transport Commission (BTC) came into existence on 1 January 1948. It acquired the railway companies (with a few small exceptions), including their docks, much of the canal system and long-distance road haulage, while the London Passenger Transport Board became one of its executives. Powers of compulsory purchase of bus and coach companies were included.

Three alternative schemes had been discussed: *regional* (with all forms of transport in a region under one authority); *territorial* (based on the four main lines and using their organisations as the basis on to which would be grafted the canals, docks and road transport); or *functional* (with separate authorities for each mode of transport). The third of these was favoured, since the ministry feared that the territorial system would lead to rail domination of other forms of transport. The industry thus came to be owned by the Commission, but it was to be managed by a body called the Railway Executive. The Commission was to have control of all its responsibilities, but the Railway Executive members were to be appointed by the minister of transport and not by the BTC – a guaranteed source of confusion for policy.

Familiar problems

From 1 January 1948 the railways were managed by a single authority, the Railway Executive. Because of the direct appointment of members of the Executive there was little opportunity for the Commission to attempt the integration of all forms of inland transport, as was expected – and is indeed expected in some quarters of government today. In practice the British Road Services Executive pressed home the advantages of road haulage for the industrial customer, taking traffic away from the railways throughout the life of the Commission. Even after the formation of the Road Passenger Executive in 1949, to take over three of the four bus groups, there was no attempt made to match rail and bus operations, with consequences to which we shall return. Railwaymen were not interested in buses; the main-line companies in the 1930s had invested in the bus industry for the sake of the dividends, but made no attempt to influence their management. In 1949 the Road Passenger Executive took up the establishment of area schemes, as required under the 1947 Act, and published its proposals for the north-east, which met with strong opposition from the municipal authorities in the area. This and other schemes were closed after the return of a Conservative administration in 1951.

The members of the Railway Executive were career railwaymen and their relationship with the Commission was fraught – so much so that they kept a specially expurgated set of minutes of their meetings which they sent to the BTC (Barker and Savage, 1974: 218). Most striking was their decision to develop a new generation of steam locomotives at a time when most European railways were converting to diesel traction, which was also the policy of the Commission.

With the return of a Conservative majority in 1951 railway policy began a process of meddling that has gone on ever since. Privatisation was not an objective, except for road haulage. The Transport Act 1953 abolished the Railway Executive and organised the industry under Area Boards whose general managers had considerable powers, and the classification and charging regulations of the 1921 Act disappeared. Costing had been little understood since the nineteenth century and only began to be analysed with the creation of the BTC Traffic-Costing Service in 1951.

Greater powers for management decision-making were clearly desirable, but the railway was still not a fully commercial organisation, its capitalisation being from the state. This being the case, the government produced the Modernisation Plan of 1955, much of which was ill thought out and even out of date. The costs involved, combined with the deficits that started to rise sharply after 1956, led to the Transport (Railway Finances) Act 1957, which authorised deficit financing to continue. A Select Committee report in 1960 criticised the economics of the modernisation schemes and recognised the virtual bankruptcy of the railways, whose operating deficit amounted to £104 million in 1962.

The practice of 'deficit financing' had started in 1956, and from that year on there was an operating loss, which was made up for by the state. Governments failed to tackle the problem. State subsidy has for long been acceptable in other countries, often by establishing, to some extent, statutory requirements that the national railway should carry various groups of people, including commuters and students (see Allen, 1996: 3). But in Britain there was no clear policy, and government merely picked up the bill for losses at the end of the financial year. Looking at this, Joy asks why, until Barbara Castle's time, governments were so open-handed; he states: 'The answer is a combination of a failure (or refusal) to understand the railways' commercial problem, pure romanticism, and the vital social need for *some* railway services' (Joy, 1973: 9).

It was plain that something had to be done, and a Bill was introduced in 1961 which became the Transport Act 1962. At the same time Ernest Marples, the Conservative minister, succeeded in attracting Dr Richard Beeching (later Lord Beeching) from his post at ICI to replace General Sir Brian Robertson as chairman of the Commission, at a salary of £24,000 in comparison with

Robertson's £10,000. Beeching became chairman of the British Transport Commission in June 1961, and there seems little doubt that his influence can be seen in the abolition of the BTC itself. The 1962 Act left the new British Railways Board under Beeching's direction, while nationalised road transport was transferred to the new Transport Holding Company. The railways had now come to attract the concentrated attention and concern of government. Road haulage, which continued to attract more and more business away from the railway, was not to arouse this kind of sentiment.

Reform and resentment

'Beeching set to work calmly and methodically' (Hardy, 1989: 11). His report, which was published on 15 March 1963, was written almost entirely by himself. It is completely objective, and contains no trace of sentimentality. In its 60 pages twice as much space is given to freight as to passenger services, yet it was the passenger policy which gave rise to an uproar the sounds of which reverberate to this day. Beeching realised quickly that there was no future for the wagon-load traffic that rumbled across the country at an average speed of 4 miles an hour, and shunting at sidings and marshalling yards had to end. Far more small goods stations were closed than those for passengers. Only bulk freight and liner trains, with the 'merry-go-round' non-stop coal trains from pit to power station, had any future, and Beeching put his weight behind their development. In 1961 freight traffic brought in more than half the railway's revenue, and all except coal was making a loss.

The closure of local goods yards met with little comment. Demand for domestic coal was diminishing, while distribution was inevitably moving to road to avoid the costs of transshipment. Marshalling yards and city goods terminals were closed and the land sold for redevelopment. Shunting locomotives were scrapped. In terms of the railway deficit none of this could happen too soon, but it signalled the end of the industry as it had existed for a hundred years, and little sentiment was aroused by the process.

The 'closure of branch lines and intermediate stations' was another matter. Closure policy turned upon two overlapping purposes, each equally abhorrent to local sentiment. First there was the case for closing little-used stations on main lines so as to improve the service between the main centres, and second there was the closure of cross-country and branch lines, mostly serving rural areas, where the operating loss was substantial. While opposition was equally strong in either case it was the closure of rural branch lines which stimulated the greatest fervour among the public, yet these, which accounted for almost a third of the railway's route mileage, could not support the variable costs of providing a train service, while they made no contribution to track costs. On the Essex branch line from Elsenham to Thaxted it would have been cheaper to provide a taxi for each passenger, yet when the last train arrived at Thaxted station, which was not even in the town, it was so full that passengers were standing in the luggage van, and it was met on arrival by crowds of people and the local brass band.

The cross-subsidy involved in providing loss-making services was such as to set train fares on intercity lines at about twice the rate of equivalent fares by coach. Beeching concluded that express coach and local bus services could readily provide the alternative to closed railway lines where they did not exist already. Few of the replacement services lasted long.

The serious problem of loss-making services took Beeching's foremost attention, but with the change of government in 1964 political thought turned to 'coordination' once more. Influenced by Frank Cousins, former general secretary of the Transport and General Workers Union and now minister of technology, Harold Wilson asked Beeching to make a broader study of both road and rail transport, but when the prime minister required the appointment of assessors rather than allowing him to produce his own report Beeching rejected the idea, and resigned as chairman of the Board on 31 May 1965 (see ibid.: 89). It is interesting to consider how his undoubted ability as a problem-solver might have laid a foundation that could have avoided the problems of the present day.

A few lines were closed that might better have survived, and some others were retained that should have gone, but the financial pressure was such that speed was essential, and much opposition and resentment could have been avoided if the process had been spread over a longer period, perhaps beginning in the 1930s. Some railway managers who had been opposed to the plan came to see that their future depended on supporting Dr Beeching, and they may have become over-enthusiastic. What the Reshaping Report did not attempt was to deal with the financial and management structure of the railway, and this was to be effectively tackled in later years by a succession of capable chairmen and managers, though the choice available was controlled by the salary limits that continued to be applied by government. What Beeching did achieve, in Gourvish's words, was that 'For the first time, the management of nationalised railways attempted to lead rather than merely respond to public political debate about the industry's future' (Gourvish, 1986: 415). How far this meant the restraint of sentiment remains to this day to be seen, but the fervour of the anti-Beeching lobby, which remains alive today, has given successive governments a constraint that will not easily be escaped.

What followed Beeching

Writing in 1965, G. Freeman Allen, editor of the journal *Modern Railways*, said of Dr Beeching: 'His outstanding achievements are to have jolted a hidebound industry out of morbid introspection into an aggressive confrontation of its competitors, to have trimmed it down to ideal fighting weight, and to have bludgeoned the public conscience into awareness of the crucial issues facing public transport in a motor age, even if the public has not yet had the courage to tackle all of them' (Allen, 1996: viii). It is open to doubt as to how far such an awareness has overcome the emotional significance of railways in the eyes of the public, even today.

One consequence of Beeching's 'reshaping' of the railway was to raise the level of political interest in public transport. Car ownership was increasing rapidly but the car was still seen largely as a middle-class extravagance. Policy was to remain wedded, as it often seems it still is, to the idea that there is public transport and there is car transport, without an appreciation that both of them form a part of the market for movement. 'Integration' became the undefined objective of public policy, replacing 'coordination'. But after a burst of activity the railway tended for a time to be left alone.

Beeching had given the Board a simpler organisation, but his successor as chairman, Stanley (later Sir Stanley) Raymond, a career railwayman, was less than successful, and in 1967 he was replaced by another railwayman, H. C. (later Sir Henry) Johnson. Barbara Castle as minister set up a Joint Steering Group, which was followed by the Transport Act 1968. This was to be the last significant piece of railway legislation until the privatisation Act of 1993, but its main concern was with road transport. It did, however, write off much of the capital debt, and it provided for the financial support of unremunerative but 'socially necessary' services.

Johnson was followed by Richard Marsh (later Lord Marsh) and then by Peter (later Sir Peter) Parker. There was friction throughout the period between the Board and the government, not least over financial limitations, but improvements were made and electrification was at last extended. The 1970s were marked by stress between the Board and successive ministers as well as by fluctuating financial objectives and provisions during a period when government was suffering from a series of macroeconomic problems. Erratic financial support and investment planning in a period of high inflation and international instability, together with severe labour problems, brought problems for all the nationalised industries, but Gourvish concludes that 'for all the talk, all the planning and strategy meetings, the rail business was suffering from drift' (Gourvish, 2002: 17). Political commentary was limited during the 1970s, perhaps reflecting a reduction in public interest in the railway problem, but attempts to raise the public image were not outstandingly successful and 'British Railways' became an object of comedy rather than respect.

In 1983 Robert (later Sir Robert) Reid became chairman, and remained in post until 1990. Government still restricted funding but passenger demand was growing, and for a time the boom in property prices meant that surplus assets could be disposed of to improve the finances of the Board. Reid was described in the trade press as 'a man of iron will, strong political awareness and strong management', and he continued the reorganisation of the railway on the basis of sectors, the regions finally disappearing in 1992.[4] The Serpell Report, *Review of Railway Finances*, which appeared in 1983, was met by strong criticism in Parliament and the media, the sound and fury illustrating once again the emotion that arises when railway policy is open to debate. It followed from criticism by Peter Parker and others concerning the need for a longer-term strategy. The Serpell committee set out to conduct a serious assessment of the state of the railway, but it was torn apart by conflict between its members as well as hostility from without, and a change of minister[5] midway through its life led to substantial changes. Not surprisingly the report had little effect, and it was shunted into the sidings. One side effect was to encourage Reid's development of sector management.

In the twenty years from 1968 there were seventeen items of transport legislation, only one of which affected the railway. (This was the Railways Act 1974, which followed a Brussels decision that the subsidy of unremunerative lines had to be provided for by a lump sum called the Public Service Obligation. Managers were known to comment that from then on the loss-making services were the railways' bread and butter.) Major intervention on the scale of 1921, 1947 or by way of privatisation was not attempted, but meddling on the part of successive ministers, fuelled by reports and studies by economists and others, was matched over the earlier part of the period by the inability of the Board to

---

4   The original sectors, later modified, were InterCity, Freight, London & South-East and Other Provincial Services, later Regional Railways.

5   David Howell replaced Norman Fowler in September 1983.

define its objectives so as to satisfy the shareholder: Her Majesty's Government. As Gourvish puts it: 'If the railways had been in the private sector the analysts would have had no hesitation in marking the shares down' (ibid.: 95). It was this situation which Sir Robert Reid confronted, with considerable success.

References

Allen, G. F. (1996), *British Rail after Beeching*, London: Ian Allan.

Bagwell, P. and P. Lyth (2002), *Transport in Britain, from Canal Lock to Gridlock*, London and New York: Hambledon.

Barker, T. C. and C. L. Savage (1974), *An Economic History of Transport in Britain*, 3rd edn, London: Hutchinson.

Bonavia, M. R. (1979), *The Birth of British Rail*, London: George Allen & Unwin.

Dyos, H. J. and D. H. Aldcroft (1969), *British Transport, an Economic Survey from the Seventeenth Century to the Twentieth*, Leicester: Leicester University Press.

Foster, C. D. (1992), *Privatization, Public Ownership and the Regulation of Natural Monopoly*, Oxford: Blackwell.

Glaister, S. and T. Travers (1993), *New Directions for British Railways? The Political Economy of Privatisation and Regulation*, London: Institute of Economic Affairs.

Gourvish, T. R. (1986), *British Railways 1948–1973 – a Business History*, Cambridge: Cambridge University Press.

Gourvish, T. R. (2002), *British Railways 1974–1997 – from Integration to Privatisation*, Oxford: Oxford University Press.

Hardy, R. H. N. (1989), *Beeching – Champion of the Railway?*, Shepperton: Ian Allan.

Joy, S. (1973), *The Train that Ran Away, a Business History of British Railways 1948–1968*, London: Ian Allan.

Miller, R. C. B. (2003), *railway.com. Parallels between the Early British Railways and the ICT Revolution*, London: Institute of Economic Affairs.

Robbins, M. (1962), *The Railway Age*, London: Routledge & Kegan Paul.

Taylor, A. J. (1972), *Laissez-faire and State Intervention in Nineteenth-century Britain* (prepared for the Economic History Society), London: Macmillan

Walker, G. (1947), *Road and Rail, an Enquiry into the Economics of Competition and State Control*, 2nd edn, London: George Allen & Unwin.

2 RAILWAYS AND THE POWER OF EMOTION: SEEKING A MARKET SOLUTION
John Hibbs

A success story forgotten

Under nationalisation, railway investment suffered from the scarcity of government financial resources and the need to satisfy the conflicting desires for investment in other government-funded services. Resources for investment came to be allocated through political rather than through market processes. Indeed, British Rail had to battle for resources even within the Ministry of Transport. In the later years of British Rail, its managers produced increased efficiency and both punctuality and reliability improved while operating costs were reduced. It was this British Rail to which the public looked back with approval after John Major's reforms came into effect; a sudden change of image that observers found it difficult to understand. Investments that were approved were managed well, so that the electrification of the East Coast Main Line was completed on time and within budget. In the 1980s the railways in this country were regarded highly in other parts of the world.

A former railwayman has looked back at those days. This was a time when governments were seeking to limit and indeed reduce public spending, and his comments are most relevant to the analysis of what happened next. He writes: 'As our sources of funding dried up we somehow managed to respond by eking out some further efficiency or eliminating another tier in the bureaucracy as we reduced operating costs (not to be confused with capital or renewals) by about 3% year after year' (John Nelson, writing in *Transit* magazine, 5 March 2004). He continues: 'It was no coincidence that the railways became more customer focussed, more punctual and more efficient in the nineties. They did so not in spite of funding cuts but because of them' (ibid.). Under Sir Robert Reid's leadership the state-owned railway built up a professionalism that looked back to the loyalty that had marked the industry from its origins while still facing the problems of the day.

Sentiment aside, British Rail, before privatisation, was functioning as well as it had ever done over the post-war years. Perhaps what we see here is a *positive* sentiment, a loyalty to 'the service', which it is only too easy for politicians to dismiss.

The path to privatisation

Politicians are thought of as reflecting public sentiment. But there is also an assumption that an incoming party in the British system will not immediately reverse the policies of its predecessor. Transport legislation continued along broadly the same lines from 1951 to 1979, except for various attempts to tackle the railway problem. The state remained in charge.

This was now to change. The new policy was to be a return to the market, and in this it challenged a range of well-established ideas about 'natural monopolies'. One such natural monopoly had long been assumed to be the telephone system, but technology had changed and the new ideas developed by Professor Stephen Littlechild enabled competition to be introduced. His concept of a regulator with positive intentions and very specific objectives came to be accepted for a range of industries, and, although modified, it has not been questioned since the Labour Party returned to power. The production and distribution of gas and electricity were reorganised in the same way, although since these had previously been in private ownership the change was less remarked. Water supply was not such an obvious candidate for privatisation, and the geography of the industry implied a territorial organisation, with local monopolies.

There seems to have been little sentimental interest on the part of the public in relation to the earlier privatisations – including in other parts of the transport industry. But railways were different. Railway privatisation was controversial even within the government and the industry itself, and with the likely loss of a majority at the next election there was pressure to complete the process, knowing perhaps that it would be an unpopular measure.

The problems facing the government were addressed in a paper delivered in 1988 to the Mont Pèlerin Society by the American economist George W. Hilton, entitled *Reconsidering Classical Objections to Laissez-faire in Railways* (published in 1990 by the Libertarian Alliance, Economic Notes no. 24). Professor Hilton identified three forms of non-competitive organisation of railways: a regulated cartel, a protected state monopoly and a subsidised state monopoly (which he identified as existing in Britain). In a telling comment on the effect on railways of growing road competition from the 1930s he concludes that in the absence of price control the railways would have become 'integrated transportation companies'. This, he says, would have had 'numerous advantages – among them, release of economists' time currently expended on studying the present organisation – but the most important would have been the centralisation of the decision on which mode of transportation to use in the hands of the entrepreneur of an integrated and competitive transportation company'. With two exceptions – freedom to engage in non-rail transportation and to withdraw from unprofitable rail services – the Railways Act 1993 followed his recommendations, but his final conclusion is telling. It is this: none of these policies for moving towards competitive organisation of transportation is without transitional difficulties, but the consequences of acceptance of the doctrine of the inherent non-competitive nature of railways as a long-term verity have been so undesirable that transitional problems are inevitable while the damage is being undone.

Whether or not the government knew of Professor Hilton's comments, their new ideas for the railways took more of the form of a regulated cartel. How far political or public opinion had recognised that a railway monopoly is meaningless in terms of the market for movement must be doubtful. The growth of low-price internal air and coach services was not foreseen at the time, but the provisions of the Railways Bill 1993 contrast with the privatisation of telecommunications, gas, air and water, in that they set up in some detail the actual structure of the privatised industry. It is as if the government was trying to design the ideal railway rather than leaving the process of the market to work things out (see also the chapter by Tyrrall in this monograph).

Reviewing the situation as the new measures were appearing, Glaister and Travers concluded that 'An informed and open discussion should take place before the start of the creation of the new market for railways. If it does not, the Government risks losing the debate without it ever having taken place' (Glaister and Travers, 1993: 64). As things happened there was very little time for a debate. The White Paper *New Opportunities for the*

Railways was published on 14 July 1992; the Commons Transport Select Committee produced critical reports on 13 January and 20 April 1993; the Bill was introduced on 22 January 1993 and, subject to minor changes, became law on 5 November 1994. The Select Committee, chaired by Robert Adley, MP, commented on the government's 'novel and untested' proposals, and observed presciently that considerable care and resources would be needed to see that the new system worked. Perhaps more relevant to the attitude of the public was Adley's remark that the effects of the Bill would be like 'a poll tax on wheels'. Looking back, *The Economist* said (3 July 1999): 'The Tories preferred to see the railway privatised badly than not at all. And that was what they got.'

The Railways Act of 1994 was a complex privatisation. While the process was to be one of de-layering, the outcome was confusing, but one thing must have been plain – that state control of the system had not been abandoned. After a relatively prosperous period British Rail was not doing well financially, so that subsidy was going to be necessary, and subsidy means oversight. Meddling was thus built into the system, and franchising combined with government subsidy encourages government intervention.

There was a range of possible approaches to privatisation.[1] These included selling the business as it stood – a solution

---

1 The present author, asked to advise the prime minister, favoured the selection of a set of privately owned operating companies, each with a territory, required by a regulator to open their tracks to other companies' trains, and working within a renewed Railway Clearing House which would have been responsible for ticketing and sales, dividing and allocating revenue by passenger mile. I was given to understand that John Major favoured the idea, but that Malcolm Rifkind, as minister of transport, turned it down because of an EU ruling that operations and infrastructure had to be separated. Strictly speaking this was intended to apply to accounting procedures only, with no requirement for structural change.

favoured by railway managers, though Nicholas Ridley is quoted as advising the prime minister that 'BR might be "a privatisation too far"' (Harris and Godward, 1997: 61). As the debate began, largely among the policy think tanks, there was little comment from the trade unions or within the Labour Party, and there is not much evidence as to how the British public felt. The confusions that eventually emerged and gave even greater opportunities for meddling can hardly be summarised as a fully rational policy, although the general objective was seen to be the greater efficiency of the industry in private ownership, together with reduced dependence upon the Treasury for investment and financial support.

After the Act the railway was open to private investment, except for the provision of 'track terminals and signalling'. There were expectations that the franchised system would enable train operating companies (TOCs) to increase efficiency so as to reduce and eventually pay back the subsidy agreed at the start of the franchise, and thus obtain some form of ownership, subject to the leasing of rolling sock. There was 'splitting the wheel from the rail' as Railtrack acquired the infrastructure before being privatised: that was the part of the process most strongly opposed by railwaymen, though it does not seem to have been an issue for the somewhat confused state of public opinion at the time.

Where public opinion and public sentiment are concerned there seems little reason to suppose that the government of the day took either matter into consideration. As the changes came into effect there was a reversion of feeling about 'British Rail' which has continued to inform journalists' attitudes ever since. Under the heading 'Return journey', *The Times* reported on 30 March 2004 that many people, according to a survey by the Rail Passengers

Council, 'believed the railways have become a national embarrassment since privatisation eight years ago'. They would prefer to return to British Rail. But there is much truth in the conclusion of *The Economist* in an article on 'Britain's rotten railways' (3 July 1999) that 'The culprit was not nationalisation itself, but the haste with which it was done'.

Government meddling – it still goes on
Rational or what?

The return of a Labour government in 1997 meant that left-wing politicians and trade unionists expected a reversal of the previous government's policies, with the renationalisation of transport, but the new government largely left things alone. Despite public misgivings the volume of travel by train increased, and the freight companies attracted new traffic from the roads. By then the ownership of the passenger train operating companies (the TOCs) had passed to holding companies, most of which had emerged from the privatisation of the bus industry in 1986. Some of them had run into problems as they de-layered management, and many of the older railwaymen took the opportunity for retirement. It began to be clear that railways are business enterprises that, because of their nature, depend upon loyalty to 'the service', which includes a respect for lessons learned from past experience. The TOCs retained respect for this, but for Railtrack and its engineering contractors there was much that needed to be relearned.

Safety is one thing that concentrates the mind of the public. This had been the concern of Her Majesty's Inspectors of Railways, who had used their powers of oversight and occasional intervention to good effect, retaining the respect of railwaymen and obtaining a significant element of insight and understanding about the way the industry worked. Few today would contest the argument that placing them within the Health and Safety Executive (HSE) was a serious mistake, and the ensuing series of accidents brought railway policy right back into public concern. There had been accidents and the occasional disaster over the years from 1830, and 100 per cent safety is never possible, but there can be little doubt that private ownership was widely held to be responsible for what came next.

Opinions may differ as to the wisdom of the Conservative government's transport policy, but while it was offensive to socialists and the trade unions it could be claimed to follow from the rational analysis of the industry in Hayekian terms. So far as the railway was concerned it could be open to criticism that some serious mistakes were made, not least the privatisation of Railtrack, which was done in a hurry and with no provision for an economic regulator of the form used in other utilities. But there seems to have been little sentiment involved, and perhaps criticism should turn upon the loss of a certain feel for the railway as an institution with its own history, traditions and loyalty. The achievements of Sir Robert Reid appear to have been forgotten.[2]

Writing in the *Sunday Times* on 14 October 2001, David Smith compared the situation of the railways with the successes of earlier privatisation, where the new companies 'were allowed time to walk before being made to run'. The problem with the privatisation of the railway was that it was too complex, and it was this which gave the new government the chance to meddle. In January

---

[2] They came to be recognised by Tom Winsor, the Rail Regulator, as he showed in his Sir Robert Reid Memorial Lecture 2004, given to the Institute of Logistics and Transport on 10 February 2004.

2004 Tom Winsor said that the meddling was 'like a virus' and, quoting his wife, who is an immunologist, he added, 'Once you have one of these things they never really go away' (*Sunday Times*, 25 January 2004).

The incoming Labour government seems to have had no clear policy for the railways, yet the events that followed were to lead to a new centralisation, perhaps more by accident than design. The first move was the formation of the Strategic Rail Authority (SRA) on 1 February 2001, with the removal of the Office of Passenger Rail Franchising. Sir Alastair Morton was appointed to run the SRA, only to resign in September 2001 and leave on 30 November 2001, not having been informed of Stephen Byers's decision to suspend Railtrack. 'Project Ariel', as it seems to have been called, was perhaps the most startling example of meddling with railway policy since the 'grouping' of 1923. The columnist John Nelson, writing in *Transit* (9 November 2001), suggested that there was a 'Basic incompatibility of a commercial monopoly in the FTSE 100 at the centre of a huge, heavily regulated public service underwritten by taxpayers' money ...'. What is less well known is the intention of Mr Byers to bring the Office of the Rail Regulator under direct political control, which was dropped after a strong protest from the chairmen of all the rail passenger operators.[3]

Meddling goes on

Just how disastrous the process of privatisation and reorganisation turned out to be has been well analysed in Christian Wolmar's book, *On the Wrong Line* (2005). His subtitle, 'How ideology and

---

3 Tom Winsor revealed this in a speech to the Centre for the Study of Regulated Industries in January 2004.

incompetence wrecked Britain's railways', can be readily justified from the story he tells. The demise of Railtrack PLC must have led any impartial observer to be disillusioned as to the rationality of the government's policy. Yet here it seems that public opinion, which is not the same thing as public sentiment, had played a part. The reaction of the media to the Ladbroke Grove and Hatfield accidents concentrated their impact, while each of them showed a different example of the weaknesses inherent in the scheme of privatisation. At Hatfield the weak regulation of Railtrack was exposed, it never having been strengthened to take account of its private ownership. Poor on-site management by Railtrack's contractors turned out to be widespread. At Ladbroke Grove the mistake in 'separating the wheel and the rail' had become apparent.[4] Ten years after privatisation the weaknesses were showing and the meddling process, fuelled now by public opinion, was intensifying. On 5 October 2001 it was manifested in a way that was both unexpected and confused when Stephen Byers activated his plan to force Railtrack into administration and to replace it with the 'not for profit company', Network Rail.

Renationalisation appeared to have been avoided, but the episode shows how far policy had come to be driven by two conflicting forces. Politically something had to be done to satisfy public and media pressure, but to take Railtrack into state ownership would bring its debts and any further subsidy on to the public balance sheet, and this the Chancellor of the Exchequer would not contemplate. It now appears that service delays became

---

4   Lateral communication within the railway could have informed the signal engineers of the badly placed signal which a low sun made it difficult for drivers to see, whereas the vertical chain of communication between the train operating company and the appropriate division of Railtrack fatally inhibited such a move.

worse under Network Rail than they had been before, and criticism mounts concerning the ability of the company's 115 members to influence the directors. There seems to have been some force in the remarks of Kim Howells, the transport minister, when he spoke at a meeting of the Fabian Society in September 2003 and accused 'trainspotters' of having an undue influence on railway policy (reported in *The Times*, 24 September 2003). Just what gives rise to the British obsession with railways, rarely to be found elsewhere, and depicted in a recent book (Marchant, 2003), is not easy to define, but the sentiment is very real and shows no sign of going away.

Just how far the secretary of state is at liberty to pursue a transport policy free of the oversight of the Chancellor has been made plain in one area where the 'trainspotters' have least influence. This is the attempt to attract freight from the roads, where the railway is but one player in the market for the movement of goods, and it is an area that has never attracted the element of railway sentiment such as we have seen to exist in the past. The 1998 White Paper *A New Deal: Better for Everyone* looked to the railway to relieve road congestion by playing a part in 'sustainable distribution'. In 2002 the 10 Year Transport Plan set a target for an 80 per cent growth rate for the rail freight sector. The rail freight companies, which are not franchised, invested substantial sums in anticipation of this, along with logistics suppliers and several of the retail chains. Planning applications were submitted for new rail-linked freight interchanges or 'hubs', such as had for some time become widespread in Italy. Some progress was made, such as the redevelopment of the former power station at Hams Hall, to the east of Birmingham, with manufacturing on site, and there was a promise of a freight spur from the main line to the

Land Rover works at Solihull. Linked to the Channel Tunnel, this would have removed a substantial quantity of traffic from the motorway, but with the increased spending on other aspects of the railway that followed after the Hatfield accident it was abandoned, along with several other proposals for new investment.

In September 2003 the SRA called for reduced maintenance on freight lines and claimed that large sums could be saved by closing sections of line for weeks at a time and banning freight trains from using parts of the network. This was an example of meddling on a gross scale, and as Frank Worsford of the University of Westminster puts it, 'Uncertainty and confusion continues [sic]' (*Logistics Manager*, December 2003/January 2004).

Meddling also continues through the influence of the HSE and is felt by all branches of the railway. It is a public authority, seemingly detached from oversight or control, whether by Parliament or by public opinion, which after its formation in 1974 incorporated the historic function of Her Majesty's Inspectors of Railways, first appointed by the Board of Trade in 1840. The influence of the HSE has been to enforce regulations that have too often been inappropriate and expensive, conflicting with the element of self-regulation proper to a fail-dangerous industry like transport. Professor David Begg is quoted as saying that while rail is ten times safer than road, 'too often the HSE is happy to see trains at a standstill rather than get decisions right' (addressing a Delivering Sustainable Rural Railways conference, January 2004).

Finally, there is a neglected area in which meddling is to be found, and it is an area in which public sentiment presents itself in a different and more political way. This is the extent of intervention open to the Scottish parliament and its executive; while such powers exist for the Welsh Regional Assembly, they are less extensive, although pressure is growing there for them to be increased. It is easy to forget the significance of railways in Scotland, where carryings outside the Strathclyde region are so thin that some 85 per cent of the network requires subsidy, and freight movement is quite small. The Scotrail franchise, funded by the Scottish Executive, seems to regard itself as having a clear political objective in showing that it can do the job better than the English. Just what this will mean for transport provision in Scotland remains to be seen, but the limited funds available to the parliament and the continued element of subsidy from the UK government would suggest that conflicting political interests will become a serious constraint upon the development of a rational transport policy for the railway or any other mode.

The confused state of railway policy today was illustrated when Tom Winsor pointed out that during his time in office as Rail Regulator there had been three secretaries of state for transport, seven ministers of transport, three permanent secretaries of the Department for Transport, two heads of the HSE, five chairmen of the infrastructure provider and two heads of the Strategic Rail Authority (interview in *The Times*, 18 October 2003).

What is so special about the railways?

The status of transport is low in the eyes of the public and the politicians, making headlines only when there is a crisis. Ministers and secretaries of state come and go, and few go on to higher positions in government. The story goes that when an MP in the 1930s was told that he was be the next minister of transport he said, 'Some enemy hath done this!' The place of the railways in the market for movement is seldom debated, and yet their importance is far less than the attention they receive would seem to warrant. Measured by volume, as we have noted, the railways account for a proportion of less than 10 per cent of the market. Wartime apart, their contribution has declined steadily since the 1920s, and yet there are those who seem to see them as in some way essential. Distribution of goods and foodstuffs today is almost entirely dependent upon road transport, and the siting of industrial and commercial business reflects this. The private car has radically changed the shape of society, with irreversible cultural consequences. The world has changed, and the railways no longer have the central importance for people and business that they had a hundred years ago. That this is obvious appears to have no effect on the attitude of the public.

Perhaps the attitude of the British to this industry, surely not equalled for any other, was reflected in a publicity campaign in the press in November 2003, when the Strategic Rail Authority took whole-page advertisements headed 'It's everyone's railway: (and you're entitled to know the facts)'. The slogan at the foot of the page, 'BRITAIN'S RAILWAY, PROPERLY DELIVERED', is clearly intended to meet the expectations of the public, but the hidden assumption must surely be 'and you've got to pay for it'. The problem remains, however, do they *want* to pay for it – even if it were properly delivered?

We have seen how strong public sentiment has been where railways are concerned. This attitude has always been distilled most effectively in the attitude of the true railway enthusiast. The railway interest is substantially wider than the bus interest, and very much larger than interest in road haulage and distribution. The railway interest should not, however, be seen as consisting merely of such enthusiasts, for there are substantial pressure groups such as the Rail Passengers Council which are well funded and which work alongside organisations such as Transport 2000 and are thus linked to the trade unions concerned. Alongside these are numerous local societies and an interest in the history of the industry extending to many branch lines and individual stations as well as the mechanical and civil engineering aspects. The serious nature of this interest is illustrated by Professor Gourvish's two substantial business histories of British Railways (Gourvish, 1986, 2002).

We have also seen the importance of loyalty to the railway as an institution, which was shown by opposition to change under the Conservative government and then by the retirement of many managers, or 'railway officers' as they were used to being known, and who saw themselves 'in the railway service'. The really successful leaders of the industry, like Sir Robert Reid, were able to combine an element close to enthusiasm with the detachment needed for effective management. The element of enthusiasm should be distinguished from popular sentiment, but put together they give rise to considerable pressure upon those responsible for public policy.

Nor is this all. We have seen the confusion of policy where the future of rail freight is concerned, which led the Rail Freight Group, the Freight Transport Association and the Confederation of British Industry to form a consortium to put pressure on the SRA and the ministry. Here we may discount the element of sentiment, which has always tended to be focused on the movement of people, but even here the consortium seeks reassurance that 'unpopular decisions are not being rushed through without proper engagement with the industry'. Beyond this there are political moves outside Westminster which raise problems for the government, whether or not they have the support of the electors. Ken Livingstone is pressing for his Transport for London (TfL) to add the suburban railways to its control, while the Passenger Transport Authorities in the conurbations are looking for some similar control over the local rail services that they subsidise, and, as we have seen, the Scottish parliament has powers that may be used to set aside some decisions made in London.

What is the future?

From 1921 to 1973 the management of the railways became increasingly centralised. Over the same period the relationship between the industry and the state became increasingly close. After 1947 the growing need for subsidy brought HM Treasury in as the *éminence grise* behind the minister of the day. Throughout the post-war years the impression seems to have grown in the minds of the public and the politicians that it was proper for the railway industry to be seen in some way as exempt from the forces of the market. Conclusions like this take time to form, but remain rooted when they are achieved. The 'great utilities' – water, gas, electricity and telephones – had been seen as natural monopolies and thus suitable for public ownership, but their privatisation was accepted as the gains that followed came to be felt. The natural monopoly argument was not seen to apply to transport as such, with even a Labour government finally withdrawing from road haulage and distribution, so how did it come about that railways were felt to be 'different' and could not be subject to market forces, for the feeling seems to remain as strong as ever?

In 1963 Sir Christopher Foster published a book called *The Transport Problem*. In it he turns to 'The Railway Problem' (Foster,

1963: 69–162). While it is set within the assumptions of a nationalised industry, Foster's chapter on 'The Railway Problem' is still worth reading, raising as it does the issues of costing and pricing that seem to be little understood to this day. Read along with Professor Gourvish's magisterial studies of the nationalised railway (Gourvish, 1986, 2002), this analysis brings to the fore all the policy issues that exist today, and from this a rational policy for the railway might be expected to follow. That such a rational policy has not been pursued is a serious criticism of the way things are done today.

However it may be driven, the development of a national policy for the transport industry, with proper concern for 'The Railway Problem', seems as far away as ever. Mr Prescott's 10 Year Plan was full of desirable objectives, but they cannot be seen to flow from a rational analysis of the issues. Integration is a buzzword meaning as little today as coordination did in the 1930s, because integration can follow only from the changing pressures of market forces; an argument that I addressed in a recent Hobart Paper (Hibbs, 2000). Professor Begg and others who are arguing today for the decentralisation of transport decision-making have a strong case, but to move the use of subsidy into the hands of regional authorities is to forget that the railways are still more of a national institution, and it is here that public sentiment continues to confuse the issue. It is the continued need for public money which brings us back to the question we asked earlier: if passengers resist higher fares, will the people accept higher taxes?

The people problem

In all organisations, some problems are so large that they are not recognised and can all too easily be ignored. Until we can step back and see the broader context we must remain confused about the more detailed objectives of policy. In the context of transport there are two such broad issues: the private car and the train.

The place of the car in our society is today a highly political issue. The initial cost of car use is low, whether the car is bought new or second hand. When the investment has been made there is an incentive to get the maximum benefit from it. When this is combined with the zero marginal price of drivers using the road, railways (and buses and trams) are at a distinct disadvantage. Furthermore, the car offers liberty of choice of destination and relative ease of travel.

There should thus be no surprise that the number of trips by train is such a small proportion of all journeys, so that for no doubt a majority of people the railway is an irrelevancy. Despite congestion, the availability of the road is taken for granted, but railways are no longer seen to be of such essential importance. Consider the response of the public if motorways were closed over the weekend for maintenance and repair, as railway lines often are today.

Sentiment is returning to the formation of railway policy, in a new and unfamiliar way. It is to be found in the high-minded pressure of what may be called the environmental movement, politically expressed with some force by the Green Party and by organisations such as Transport 2000. It is a sentiment that can only be described as anti-car, seeking to condemn those who choose to use personal transport and are therefore seen to be selfish and immoral. The broader problem here is something that these lobbyists fail to see, preferring to advocate the increasingly severe limitation of freedom of choice. Their essentially middle-class approach forgets that some 40 per cent of cars are now owned by working-class families, among whom multi-car ownership is increasingly common. Having a car is, after all, the best way of setting out to get a better job. Lack of access to a car is a constraint for many older people, but it is the bus rather than the train which can help there.

The impact of this political pressure, based as it is upon feeling as much as fact, cannot but influence railway policy. It leads to arguments in favour of subsidy and for the continued operation of loss-making sections of line. Yet the arguments essentially bypass consideration of freight train operators. Emotions are heated whenever it is suggested that the railway is superfluous, and that the system, London suburban lines perhaps apart, might well be shut down. Articles about the Japanese bullet trains command headlines, and there is still a belief that the French run better trains then the British, which is, to say the least, disputable. For some reason the iconic nature of the train is limited to the movement of people, few of whom actually use it. Proposals for a new freight-only line from the north of England through the Midlands to the Channel Tunnel with dedicated access have been resisted strongly by the same environmentalists who wish to promote greater movement of people by rail. It is the passenger train which seems to be admired and defended, along with the assumed superiority of anything that runs on rails, such as a tram. The social status of the bus is very much lower.

The flourishing activity of the Association of Community-Rail Partnerships in seeking to maintain local railways even where demand is limited illustrates the *meaning* of the train in our society. But such sentiment should not be the main driver of policy.

Conclusion

Contemplating the failure of the 1968 Transport Act, Pryke and Dodgson (1975) blamed the weakness of the post-Beeching British Railways Board and the intransigence of the railway trade unions. Under the chairmanship of Sir Robert Reid much was done to improve the management of the business, but their conclusion still rings true today. Here is what they said then (ibid.: 275–6):

> Another even more important requirement if a rational policy for the railways is to be adopted is that there should be a change in public opinion. At present, both among public leaders and large sections of the general public, railways are viewed as a necessary public service, and this catch phrase is thought to be a cogent argument for massive investment, low fares and the preservation of each and every branch line. Whatever is the truth of the matter, railways today seem still to be seen as a national necessity, and not as just one player in the market for movement.

In the words of the same authors, 'Production can only be regarded as socially necessary so long as the benefits, both public and private, are greater than the costs incurred' (ibid.: 274–5). Instead, public opinion seems to have assumed for a long time that British Railways was a sort of public charity, such as the National Health Service, at least so far as its passenger trains were concerned. As we saw earlier, this is nothing new, having been stated in the press as early as 1886. This idea does not seem to have gone away despite privatisation, although only the boldest have gone so far as to ask whether we would be better off today if railways had never been invented.

It is here that transport policy continues to pander to public sentiment. So long as the economics of the motor industry and the zero marginal cost of road use press down the balance on the side of the private car, while at the same time public opinion seeks to preserve the train, a meaningful measure of 'the benefits, both public and private' is manifestly hard, perhaps impossible, to achieve. Public sentiment such as this must make it difficult to see the railway as just another kind of business. The function of the Department for Transport is subdivided between the various modes: road, rail, air and water. But an economically sound policy for the railway must be part of a rational policy across all modes, however difficult that may be, and today's mix of anti-car and pro-train sentiment simply makes the problem worse. But this is nothing new.

Over the whole spectrum of opinion today the railway appears to be seen as something special – not quite a business to be managed efficiently, but perhaps rather a toy to be played with. Safety regulation is a government responsibility, but running trains is best left to companies whose managers seek to satisfy demand in a competitive industry. Yet over the years governments have interfered with the railway, and demonstrated their inability to understand what the business is about, while the outcome has invariably been detrimental to the economy and to the consumers.

References

Foster, C. D. (1963), *The Transport Problem*, London: Blackie & Son (revised edn, London: Croom Helm, 1974).

Glaister, S. and T. Travers (1993), *New Directions for British Railways? The Political Economy of Privatisation and Regulation*, London: Institute of Economic Affairs.

Gourvish, T. R. (1986), *British Railways 1948–1973 – a Business History*, Cambridge: Cambridge University Press.

Gourvish, T. R. (2002), *British Railways 1974–1997 – from Integration to Privatisation*, Oxford: Oxford University Press.

Harris, N. G. and E. Godward (1997), *The Privatisation of British Rail*, London: Railway Consultancy Press.

Hibbs, J. (2000), *Transport Policy, the Myth of Integrated Planning*, London: Institute of Economic Affairs.

Marchant, I. (2003), *Parallel Lines, or Journeys on the Railway of Dreams*, London: Bloomsbury.

Pryke, R. W. S. and J. S. Dodgson (1975), *The Rail Problem*, London: Martin Robinson.

Wolmar, C. (2005), *On the Wrong Line*, London: Aurum Press.

PART TWO

WHO SHOULD RUN THE RAILWAYS? AN ASSESSMENT OF RAILWAY PRIVATISATION

3 THE RESTRUCTURING OF THE RAIL SYSTEM IN BRITAIN – AN ASSESSMENT OF RECENT DEVELOPMENTS

Rico Merkert[1] and Chris Nash

Introduction

In July 2004 the British government published its White Paper *The Future of Rail* (DfT, 2004), proposing major changes in the structure of the railway industry. As the British rail industry was fundamentally transformed in 1994, in 2001 and is being transformed again, the focus of this chapter will be questions about potential problems with the various systems. Because the British rail privatisation is now relatively well known, our review of the privatisation process will be relatively short and we will concentrate our attention on the current system and recent developments. To assess whether all the structural changes were necessary and effective the chapter will also draw on published statistical material to examine significant trends in the performance of Britain's railways. The literature and empirical findings are informed by interviews with key people associated with the industry and by reference to submissions to the 2004 rail structure review. This

---

[1] This paper was prepared during a Research Fellowship at the Institute for Transport Studies, University of Leeds, supported by the Human Resources and Mobility Programme 'Marie Curie' of the European Union. An earlier version was presented at 'INFRATRAIN Autumn School 2004' at Berlin University of Technology. The authors acknowledge helpful comments from Jeremy Toner and Andrew S. J. Smith and two anonymous referees. Any remaining errors are the responsibility of the authors.

chapter examines the main problems that led the government to publish the White Paper and takes a critical view of the resulting measures, such as the abolition of the Strategic Rail Authority (SRA).

The privatisation process

The British railway system is not known only as the most liberalised railway system in Europe (see IBM and Kirchner, 2004), but sometimes also as an example that shows how the privatisation of network industries can bring problems as well as advantages.

Following a series of privatisations in Britain, carried out by successive Conservative administrations, railways were the last network sector to be privatised, and probably the most complex. The biggest problem faced by British Rail (BR), and the main reason for selling off its non-core businesses, was the weak profitability of the railways (Welsby and Nichols, 1999: 56). Since the 1950s Britain's railways have been in a loss-making position, largely dependent on government subsidies. At the same time the railway's market share both in passenger and in freight has been in long-term decline. Although Cowie (2002: 34) reveals that efficiency of the railways had improved between 1985 and 1990, the government still argued that the performance of BR was inadequate. The government's aims in the railway privatisation process, as stated in the White Paper *New Opportunities for the Railways* (DTp, 1992), were: to make better use of the railways, to ensure greater responsiveness to the customer, to provide higher quality of service, and to provide better value for money. The key to success in achieving these aims was seen to be improving reliability and efficiency, and strengthening the financial position of the industry. The introduction of competition through greater involvement of the private sector and ending BR's monopoly in the operation of services was the proposed instrument for achieving this: 'Introducing competition, innovation and the flexibility of private sector management will enable the railways to exploit fully all the opportunities open to them' (ibid.).

Because the British rail reform is now widely known and exhaustively discussed in the existing literature, this section will provide only a brief description of the steps undertaken by the British government. Between 1994 and 1997 the organisational structure of the rail industry was fundamentally rebuilt (Kain, 1998, and Harris and Godward, 1997, provide comprehensive overviews). The principal change was the separation of BR's infrastructure from its transport operations. A new government-owned company, Railtrack, took over ownership and management of BR's railway infrastructure in 1994. All other BR activities were split into more than one hundred companies and then transferred to the private sector, mainly by tendering. Railtrack was sold in 1996 to the private sector through flotation on the stock market, following the model of a regulated private infrastructure monopoly. Railtrack staff undertook signalling and control, but did not carry out engineering tasks. For those tasks, mainly infrastructure renewal and maintenance, the approach was to subcontract to former BR units, which became individual private companies. To introduce more competition and reduce market entry barriers the other essential asset, rolling stock, was sold off to three private Rolling Stock Companies (ROSCOs).

For the operations, a franchise model with 25 train-operating companies (TOCs) was chosen for passenger transport, while the freight operations were sold off as Freight Operating Companies

(FOCs). While access to the franchised passenger market was regulated, there was open access in the freight market. As part of the reform two regulatory bodies were created. The Office of Rail Regulator (ORR) was responsible for economic regulation and focused mainly on Railtrack as the monopoly player of the industry, setting track access charges and conditions as well as having the power to impose licence conditions. The Office of Passenger Rail Franchising (OPRAF) was primarily responsible for awarding franchises and, through the franchises, for paying subsidies as well as regulating the TOCs, including controlling some fares. Safety regulation was given to the Health and Safety Executive (HSE), to which the Railways Inspectorate (HMRI) was transferred. As a result, there have been three bodies involved in regulation, in order to separate the roles of economic and safety regulation from the process of determining subsidy levels, and in theory they each had distinctive responsibilities. This regulatory structure was completed with a complex set of compensation regimes between the TOCs and Railtrack and between OPRAF and the TOCs.

When Labour came to power in 1997, it announced changes in policy and administration. In its 10 Year Transport Plan (DETR, 2000), Labour envisaged a 50 per cent increase in passenger traffic and an 80 per cent increase in freight traffic. Given that there had already been substantial increases in rail traffic since privatisation, the network was faced with scarce capacity. The Labour Party expected enormous investments, especially from the private sector, to enhance the network, which was ambitious and, as Glaister (2002) shows, in no way achieved. To realise this fundamental growth, the responsibility of OPRAF was expanded to take on a strategic role in planning and investment, and in 2001 it was renamed the Strategic Rail Authority (SRA). The purpose of the SRA was, according to a government White Paper in 1998, to provide 'a clear, coherent and strategic programme for the development of our railways' (DETR, 1998). Although there had been substantial cost savings and performance improvements (Pollitt and Smith, 2002), there were also a number of problems apparent with the original privatisation.

One source of problems during the early post-privatisation period was the over-achievement of one of the aims of the rail reform. Growth in passenger as well as in freight markets was much more than anticipated. At the same time the industry was faced with problems related to service quality, investment and profitability, and perceived problems in the area of safety and profitability (Nash, 2002). In the first franchise round the TOCs with the lowest subsidy requirements generally succeeded. Some TOCs therefore had ambitious revenue targets and others were building their franchise bids around big reductions in operating cost. The TOCs had in both cases a strong interest in increasing their revenue. Because almost 50 per cent of the fares were regulated (RPI price-capped), and because the marginal costs of train operation were low, owing to the 91 per cent fixed part of the track access charges (Crompton and Jupe, 2003: 405), the TOCs increased the train kilometres on the network, which was already at its capacity limit on certain lines. On the other hand Railtrack had no incentives to enable the TOCs to operate more trains on its network. One reason for that was the structure of the track access charges; another was the complex penalty regime that was part of the track access agreements. Railtrack was forced to compensate the TOCs for performance below a certain level, and more trains on the network meant an increased probability that Railtrack could not provide that level of service. In its Periodic Review the ORR (2000) made a major change to the incentive structure to realign the interests of Railtrack with those of the TOCs. To incentivise Railtrack to facilitate growth on the network, the proportion of variable charges (including a new capacity charge) was increased to 20 per cent, and an incentive payment to Railtrack directly linked to traffic growth was introduced.

At the same time some of the TOCs got into financial trouble. Instead of allowing some of them to go bankrupt the SRA moved those franchises to management contracts with increased subsidies. These management contracts were always seen as a temporary measure, but changing franchising policy and the post-Hatfield crisis prolonged their life.

To sum up, although there were some sceptics, especially regarding vertical separation (see, e.g., Preston, 1996) and privatisation (Wolmar, 2001), it is now acknowledged that the early post-privatisation experience was better than expected by many people (see, e.g., Pollitt and Smith, 2002). Preston (1999) draws twenty lessons from the British rail reform, the majority being positive. He highlights the positive effects of the (although limited) on-the-track competition, such as product differentiation, increased service frequency and selective fare cuts. Van de Velde et al. (1998) point out that there have been important entrepreneurial initiatives since privatisation, with the most important concerning marketing and ticketing. Nash (2004) concludes that the industry structure adopted at privatisation was the best way of introducing competition to the railways. The new structure clearly increased complexity and created some problems, owing mainly to its rushed implementation and mostly related to contractual design. Additionally these problems have to be weighted against the benefits of competition. In total the increased performance, the growth in traffic and the achieved cost savings outweigh the problems faced between 1994 and 2000.

The problems of Railtrack

Because many of the difficulties of railway reform were related to the infrastructure manager, this section will provide a brief introduction to the weaknesses of Railtrack and its successors.

As mentioned above, Railtrack subcontracted all its maintenance and renewal activities and the maintenance and renewal companies subcontracted many tasks as well. There were at one point more than two thousand subcontractors, and the infrastructure manager lost skilled engineering staff and valuable information about the condition of the infrastructure (Grayling, 2001: 23). In Lord Cullen's report on railway safety (Cullen, 2001), the poor management of the maintenance and renewal contracts by Railtrack is highlighted too, and it is concluded that better coordination, clearer lines of accountability and fewer subcontractors are desirable, but vertical integration is not a necessary prerequisite for this. Already, the accident at Ladbroke Grove had led to concern about safety, and finally the Hatfield accident changed the whole story of the British rail reform. In order to avoid every risk, with poor understanding of the condition of the network but knowing that the cause for the accident was a broken rail, every metre of the network was inspected for gauge-corner cracking, which led to a multitude of re-railing initiatives and temporary speed restrictions, 'just in case' anything was wrong (Foster, 2005). By doing this, Railtrack restricted the ability of the TOCs to run their advertised timetables, and freight, as well as passenger travel, temporarily collapsed (passenger numbers fell by up to 40 per cent; CfIT, 2001). As a result, Railtrack was obliged to pay more than £500 million in compensation to train operators (Kennedy and Smith, 2004: 158). At the same time, the cost of the upgrade of the West Coast Line went out of control and escalated from an initial estimate of £2.3 billion in 1996 to £5.8 billion in 2000 (ORR, 2000). All these costs undermined Railtrack's finances, devastated its share price and compromised its capacity to raise capital. Hence Railtrack was forced to request direct financial support from the government, and as the offered funding (£1.5 billion under various conditions) was thought to be not enough, the government withdrew support for Railtrack and placed it in administration in October 2001 (Shaw et al., 2003: 148).

The administrators of Railtrack plc – the accountancy firm Ernst & Young – planned to run the company as normally as possible while it was under their control. During that time there was a politically driven demand for massive safety improvements on the network, and the huge volume of work led to bottlenecks and increases in prices. As a result, the maintenance and renewal costs increased dramatically during the time of administration (see Table 1). In October 2002, a new company, Network Rail (NR), purchased Railtrack, and this company now owns and manages the infrastructure. This not-for-dividend company is limited by guarantee and its members are stakeholders rather than shareholders. Network Rail has a profit motive but it reinvests any profit, instead of paying a dividend to its members. The decision to place Railtrack into administration, and replace it with a not-for-dividend company, may have weakened incentives for cost control at a critical time for the industry.

The British infrastructure manager has seen three different

Table 1 **Cost of maintenance, operation and renewal of the rail network (£ billion, 2002/03 prices)**

Regulator's determination for control period 1 (5 yrs)	14
Regulator's determination for control period 2 (5 yrs)	16.7
Control period 2 revised by Railtrack plc	
– summer 2001	21.8*
Control period 2 revised by Railtrack in administration (5 yrs)	
– March 2002	26.3
– October 2002	28.5
Control period 2 revised by Network Rail (5 yrs)	
– October 2002	26.1
– March 2003	27.7
– June 2003	27.1
Regulator's determination for 2004/05–2008/09 (5 yrs), as at December 2003	22.2†

Sources: Network Rail Business Plan Update (June 2003); ORR Access Charges Review, Final Conclusions, December 2003

* Based on regulator's determination for control period 2, plus an additional £5.1 billion requested by the company (£1.5 billion for RenewCo, and an extra £3.6 billion announced later in the summer of 2001)

† Note that this funding covers the period 2004/05–2008/09, whereas control period 2 covers the period 2001/02–2005/06

ownership models within less than ten years, and many difficulties in the British rail reform were related to the infrastructure. Key findings of a Mercer Management Consulting and DTLR (2002) study, which are mainly based on more than fifty interviews with key persons in the industry and related professionals, reveal four major problems, all related to the infrastructure manager and a general lack of consideration of value for money. They point out the failure to implement maintenance and renewal of the network correctly, stemming from a loss of knowledge and expertise, compounded by historic under-investment. Furthermore they highlight the poor investment planning and strategies, the inefficient capacity utilisation on a congested network and the onerous and bureaucratic concern for safety without a balancing cost–benefit analysis of safety regulation. To get cost and the maintenance difficulties under control, NR has recently taken maintenance back in house.

To sum up, there have been difficulties with management of the rail infrastructure. Most of them were caused, however, by management failures and weak incentives. It is not clear that they were fundamental flaws in the structure which could not have been remedied by the combination of improved contractual relationships, redesigned track access charges and leadership on planning and investment from the SRA.

Performance since 1994

Figure 1 shows that both passenger and freight traffic grew rapidly in the early years post-privatisation, although this was partly a result of cyclical movements of the economy. The Hatfield accident and the resulting disruption temporarily halted that growth, but since then the number of passenger kilometres (Pkm) has been climbing again and reached a record number in 2003 of more than 40.9 billion (SRA, 2004a).

Given the growth in traffic, it might be expected that scarcity of capacity on the network would cause a fall in punctuality. Figure 2 shows that in fact punctuality improved post-privatisation. There are two measures illustrated in the figure. This is because the Shadow Strategic Rail Authority (SSRA) – now the SRA – introduced a new Public Performance Measure (PPM) in June 2000 to give a better indication of the actual performance of Britain's passenger railways. The PPM combines figures for punctuality and reliability into a single performance measure. Unlike the replaced

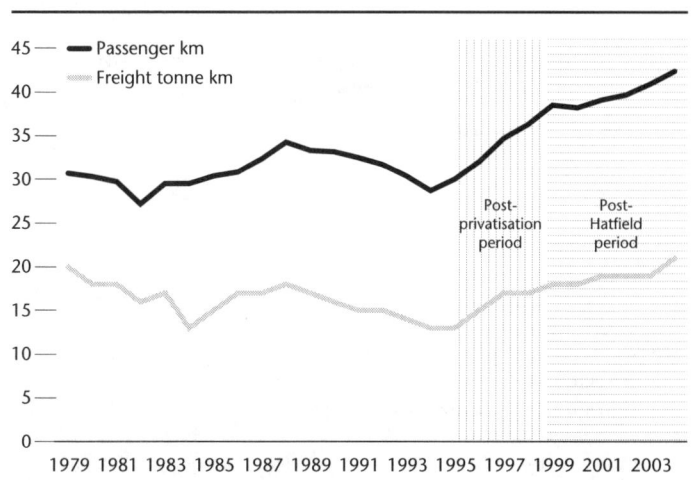

Figure 1 **Rail passenger and freight volumes**
Billions, 1979–2002/03

- Passenger km
- Freight tonne km

Post-privatisation period

Post-Hatfield period

Sources: Dft (2002); SRA (2004a)

Charter Punctuality Measure, it covers all scheduled services, seven days a week. The PPM measures the performance of individual trains against their planned timetable and is therefore the percentage of trains 'on time' (within five minutes for regional trains and ten minutes for long-distance trains) compared with the total number of trains planned.

Figure 2 also reveals, however, that the Hatfield accident had a strong negative impact on the punctuality of trains and that since then the percentage of trains on time has been recovering rather slowly. Although there have been improving numbers in the last two years, the level of punctuality still remains below pre-Hatfield levels.

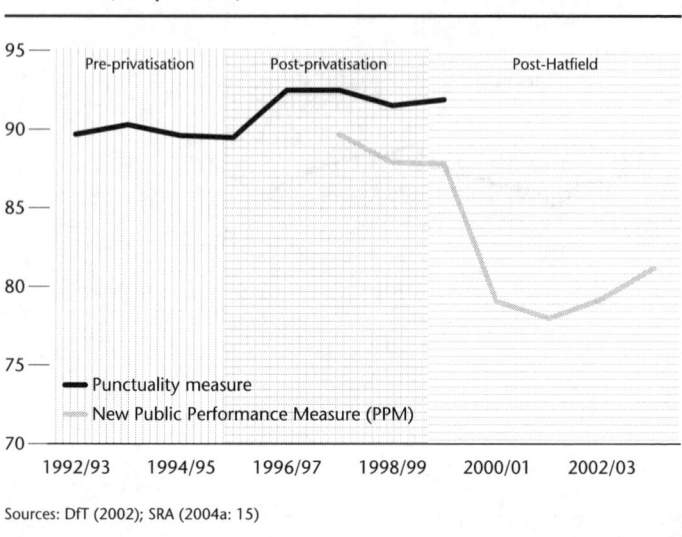

Figure 2 **Punctuality: percentage of trains arriving on time (all operators)**

Pre-privatisation | Post-privatisation | Post-Hatfield

— Punctuality measure
— New Public Performance Measure (PPM)

Sources: DfT (2002); SRA (2004a: 15)

The quality-related performance indicator with the most publicity in Britain is safety. There have been several serious rail accidents in the UK since 1994. Those with the highest number of fatalities and therefore with most public awareness have been Ladbroke Grove on 5 October 1999, with thirty-one fatalities, Hatfield on 17 October 2000, with four fatalities, Selby on 28 February 2001 with ten fatalities, Potters Bar on 10 May 2002 with seven fatalities, and most recently near Reading, Berkshire, on 11 November 2004 with six fatalities. Investigators found evidence that the last accident at the Berkshire level crossing was caused by a motorist committing suicide, and that at Selby was due to a motor vehicle falling on to the track, but in Hatfield and Potters

Figure 3 **Number of significant train incidents**
Per million train kilometres

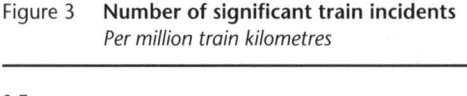

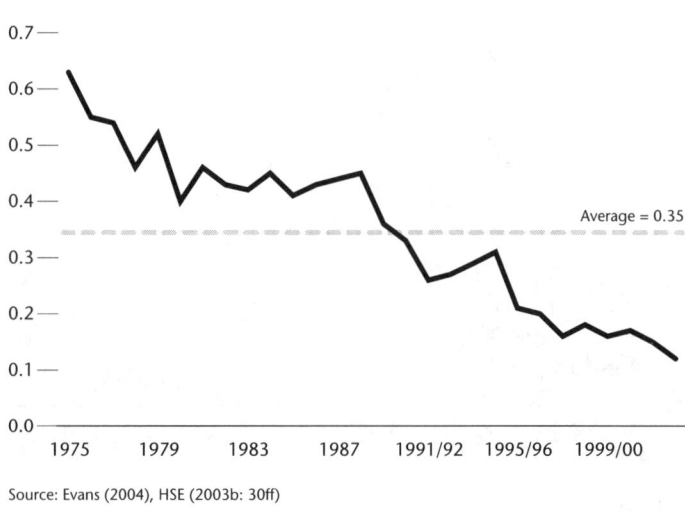

Source: Evans (2004), HSE (2003b: 30ff)

Bar poorly maintained infrastructure was the most likely cause for the derailments (see, e.g., HSE, 2003a). This might provide an argument suggesting that there were weak incentives to maintain the network post-privatisation, but if one looks at historical data it becomes obvious that train accidents happened before privatisation too. Two examples are the Polmont accident on 30 July 1984 with thirteen fatalities, and the accident at Clapham Junction on 12 December 1988 with thirty-five fatalities. In the latter case, faulty signalling was found to be responsible. In respect of the number of significant train incidents per train kilometre, initial statistical analysis of accidents revealed that safety was not worse post-privatisation (see HSE, 2003b; Evans, 2000, 2004). Figure

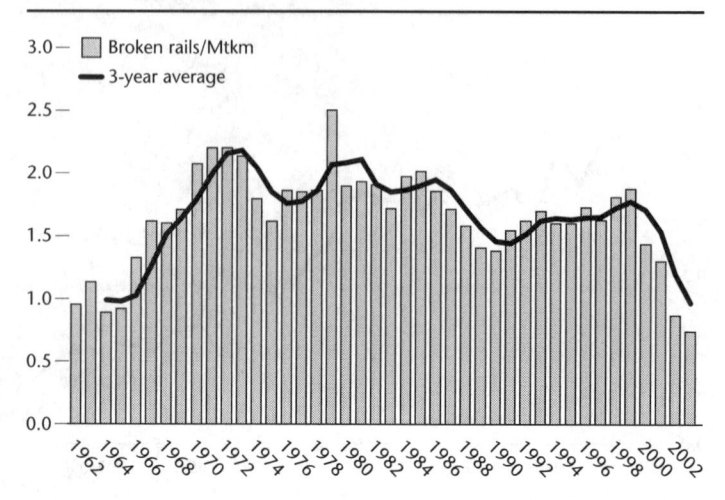

Figure 4 **Number of broken rails**
Per million train kilometres (Mtkm)

Source: Network Rail/RSSB

3 illustrates an improvement in safety performance, and Evans (2004) concludes that safety has improved faster since privatisation than under British Rail for all classes of accidents.

As the crucial Hatfield accident was caused by a broken rail, it seems sensible to analyse how the number of broken rails per train kilometre has changed over time. Figure 4 indicates that there was a peak post-privatisation, but that there have been even higher peaks pre-privatisation. Rail breaks have more than halved since 1999, as a result of massive renewal activities. In 2003, the number (380) and the rate (0.74 broken rails per million train kilometres) were the lowest for 40 years, and that can be seen as an indication of the better quality of the tracks. Whether in fact the level of

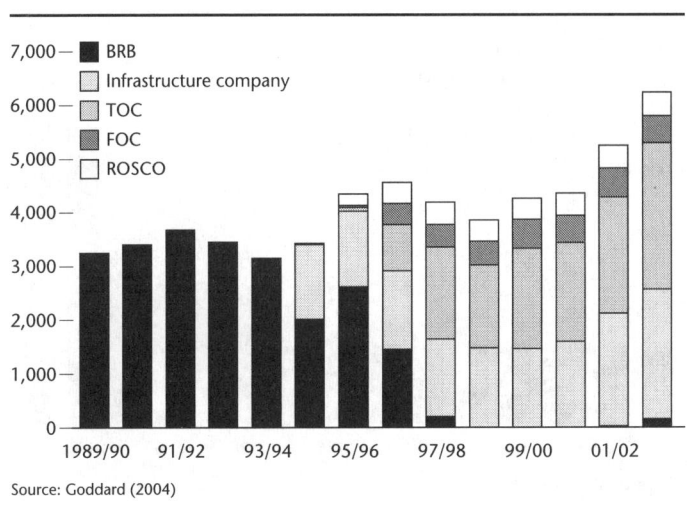

Figure 5 **Rail industry operating costs**
1989/90–2002/03, £ 2002/03 millions

- BRB
- Infrastructure company
- TOC
- FOC
- ROSCO

Source: Goddard (2004)

expenditure necessary to achieve this reduction was justified does, however, remain open to doubt.

The White Paper (DfT, 2004) identified the increasing cost of the rail industry as one of the main problems. To examine sources of potential cost increases we will distinguish between operating cost and capital expenditure. As Figure 5 illustrates, there has been a rapid increase in total rail industry operating cost per train kilometre since the Hatfield rail accident. All elements of cost seem to have increased (see Smith, 2006).

It is widely argued that there had been under-investment in Britain's railways immediately before privatisation and during the Railtrack era as well, creating a need for increased renewal activity (with the high volumes of track renewed in the 1970s now

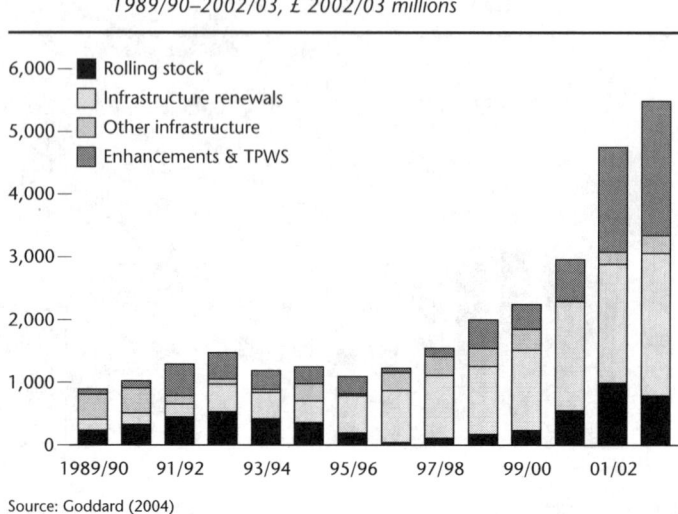

Figure 6   **Rail industry capital expenditure**
1989/90–2002/03, £ 2002/03 millions

- Rolling stock
- Infrastructure renewals
- Other infrastructure
- Enhancements & TPWS

Source: Goddard (2004)

becoming due again for renewal). Capital expenditure increased substantially by £4.6 billion in nominal terms between 1989/90 and 2002/03, with the increase occurring primarily in recent years. Some major projects, such as the West Coast Line, displayed massive cost increases as against budget. Figure 6 shows that the increase in capital expenditure is mainly due to infrastructure renewals and enhancements (including the implementation of the Train Protection and Warning System (TPWS)), but there has also been an increase in capital expenditure for rolling stock.

More recent data for investment in rail, published by the SRA (2004a: 51), indicate investment of £5.496 billion in total and £774 million for rolling stock for the year 2003/04. The peak year for rolling-stock investment was 2001/02, but even

Table 2 **Government support to the rail industry (£m)**

Year	Central government grants	PTE grants	Direct rail support	Other elements of government support	Freight grants	Total government support
1985–86	849	78	0	61	7	995
1986–87	755	70	0	22	6	853
1987–88	796	68	0	−251	2	615
1988–89	551	70	0	−175	2	448
1989–90	479	84	0	232	1	796
1990–91	637	115	0	440	4	1,196
1991–92	902	120	0	562	1	1,585
1992–93	1,194	107	0	870	2	2,173
1993–94	926	166	0	535	4	1,631
1994–95	1,815	346	0	−464	3	1,700
1995–96	1,712	362	0	−1,643	4	435
1996–97	1,809	291	0	−1,044	15	1,071
1997–98	1,429	375	0	25	29	1,858
1998–99	1,196	337	0	53	29	1,615
1999–00	1,031	312	0	75	23	1,441
2000–01	847	283	0	84	36	1,250
2001–02	731	306	684	105	57	1,883
2002–03	935	304	1,166	183	49	2,637

Source: SRA (2004a: 47)

Note: Other elements of government support include lending to finance investment and receipts from the sale of assets

today the investment in rolling stock is much higher than before privatisation.

A key question for policy-makers is how to rearrange the framework to provide incentives to the industry to deliver the right balance between safety and all the other performance parameters at reasonable cost – or, in other words, how to deliver value for money. A second question is how much money the state should provide. Table 2 indicates government support to the rail industry since 1985/86. It is important to mention that the form of privatisation led to higher government grants in the short term. All assets were sold off and train-operating companies suddenly had to pay commercial rates for using them. Therefore the revenue support grants to domestic passenger services (central government grants plus Passenger Transport Executive (PTE) grants) increased sharply directly after privatisation. The amount of subsidies then declined, but not by as much as expected, partially because of the financial difficulties of some TOCs. Renegotiation of these contracts plus the cost effects of Hatfield led government support to the rail industry to increase enormously.

To sum up, following privatisation there was a promising start with rail traffic volumes increasing rapidly, improvements in performance, increasing investment and cost savings. Despite a widespread misperception, safety continued to improve. The two really problematic indicators are the dramatically increasing costs and weak punctuality since the Hatfield accident.

The rail structure review

The government has been well aware of the problems of weak performance and cost escalation, and saw an urgent need to understand the reasons for recent cost rises and to trim costs and subsidies. Therefore the government initiated a review of the industry in January 2004 and invited key players to submit their views. The results of the review were published in the White Paper *Future of Rail* (DfT, 2004). The government identified ten specific problems:

1   There is a lack of accountability and of clear strategic direction.

2   The SRA as a public sector body cannot lead the industry from within and there are limits to its ability to set the strategic agenda for the railways.
3   The SRA is responsible only for a single mode of transport and therefore has no flexibility to make changes within the wider transport budget to reflect changing priorities.
4   There is too much fragmentation of responsibilities in the public sector.
5   There is no binding arrangement between the government and Network Rail.
6   There is a lack of any single body with operational responsibility which would automatically assume leadership of major projects.
7   ORR determines the output and price of Network Rail's work. In addition the TOCs are insulated from the effects of increasing track access charges through their franchise contracts. As a result, the government has no control over the subsidies to rail and is not able to control the level of public funding.
8   Relationships that are too complex and bureaucratic lead to longer reaction time (the system is unable to react quickly because consensus between Network Rail, freight operators and TOCs is needed – for example, in dealing with incidents, timetable changes) and everyone is just passing the buck, rather than working in partnerships.
9   There is a very inefficient penalty payment regime.
10 Ticket revenues are inefficiently allocated to train companies (by number of services run, rather than by number of passengers).

The government attempted to remedy these problems in the following ways.

In response to the first four points, the government took direct charge of setting the strategy and the level of public expenditure for the railways, abolishing the SRA. All functions regarding strategic planning and franchising moved to the Department for Transport (DfT), because the government wished to have direct political control over an industry receiving such enormous subsidies. It is, however, questionable whether the government did not have this control already (see, e.g., Shaw, 2004). As a result of the Transport Act 2000 the SRA was the instrument of the government. The DfT had overall control of strategic direction and for every strategy the SRA had to have the specific approval of the Secretary of State for Transport. Glaister (2004) feared that the abolition of the SRA would lessen the degree of transparency within the rail system. He points out that the SRA as a separate public body published annual reports, which the DfT is probably not going to do.

It is intended that local authorities (the PTEs) in major cities will have responsibility for apportioning subsidies between different modes of public transport and that London, Scotland and Wales will be granted greater power. The effects of this move might be that the government will shift some financial responsibilities towards the PTEs and that as a result there will be some replacement of rail by bus services, because buses are overall much cheaper than railways. The regional Rail Passenger Committees, which could oppose potential line closures at a regional and local level, will be abolished, while the Rail Passenger Council will champion passenger concerns both regionally and nationally.

In response to points 5, 6 and 8, Network Rail will be the responsible body for the performance of the rail network through a new binding agreement with the government. Subsequent debate has revealed, however, that this 'new' binding agreement will be nothing more than the Network Code and revised network licence conditions, so how new it is may be debated. Furthermore the number of franchisees will be reduced and they will be aligned more closely with Network Rail's regional structure. The objective of this proposed measure is to enhance local responsibility and to enable Network Rail and the TOCs to work more closely together. It is widely seen as sensible to reduce the number of franchises, in order to improve capacity utilisation, although this will lead to less competition in the market. Earlier reductions in franchises have lessened the already limited competition within the market (for example, between Thames and Great Western on the route section Paddington–Reading–Didcot). The benefits of less fragmentation are nevertheless expected to outweigh the losses of potentially less competition. As a result of the large size of franchises, however, the entry barriers for small TOCs will increase, owing to higher financial requirements for running the business and for putting a bid together for such a franchise (Bastow, 2004).

The other functions of the SRA, such as developing route utilisation strategies (as well as planning minor enhancements of the network), have also passed to Network Rail. As a result, Network Rail has almost complete control of day-to-day operations. Once the timetable is set up the TOCs will not have the right to add extra services, and Network Rail will be able to cut services if it considers that they interfere with its duty to maintain the tracks.

Point 7 is a key point and the subject of much debate. Winsor (2004), who was regulator at the time of the post-Hatfield cost explosion, argues that the government always had the option of determining its spending on railways, but that if it wanted to spend less than the regulator believed to be necessary to maintain the current planned outputs then it would have to cut its output requirements. The government has tried to make this process more transparent, in terms of an iterative process to ensure that the outcome of reviews of track access charges are consistent with government expenditure plans. This will not, however, make the choice between increased expenditure and cutting services any more politically palatable.

There are no specific proposals regarding points 9 and 10. While a simpler performance regime may be desirable, there seems little doubt that an appropriate regime is crucial to provide incentives to the various parties in the industry. Point 10 is actually misleading; revenue is currently allocated in accordance with a computer programme that predicts which trains passengers will catch; TOCs have the right to demand a survey if they dispute the results, but they have to pay for it.

From an economic point of view, perhaps the most sensible measure is the transfer of HMRI to the ORR. The ORR covers safety, performance and cost and within this single institution can try to examine the right balance between these three factors. It is largely agreed that this move will increase the efficiency of rail regulation. Nevertheless there are concerns regarding possible conflicts of interest. It is furthermore planned to provide rail freight with long-term certainty over access to the network, and to identify a group of key routes on which freight operators will enjoy and pay for more assured rights of access. This measure will possibly mean that in the future FOCs will also pay, to some extent, a fixed part of the track access charges, increasing costs for freight on rail, which as a result could lead to a shift to road transport.

Thus it may be seen that, despite giving the impression of major changes to correct serious flaws in the structure of the industry, the White Paper did not affect any of the main characteristics of the British rail system, such as vertical separation, franchising of passenger services, open access for freight and independent regulation. In order to learn what other people believe the problems of the industry and their solutions to be, interviews with key people associated with the industry and a review of submissions of some key interested parties to the 2004 railway structure review will inform the analysis below.

As Foster (2005) points out, one of the weaknesses of the initial reform was the way the government rushed privatisation through. He argues that there were not many fundamental problems with the proposed structure but a lot of problems with the implementation of that structure. With respect to the 2004 White Paper it has to be asked whether the DfT's conclusions and proposed changes are too rushed and what the implementation will look like.

The SRA (2004b) tells a positive story in its submission to the rail review: 'Britain's railway is now rehabilitated and ready for real delivery to passengers and investors alike. There is now stability, clarity and certainty around major projects and train franchising, where before there was drift, doubt and confusion.' As outlined above, there are problems with the current system, and most other people who handed in a submission, such as Foster and Castles (2004), see Britain's railways as being in a mess.

The first critical question one could ask is why the government is abolishing an agency just three years after installing it, and whether this could lead to even greater political interference.

One of the general problems of the British rail reform was that in rail, unlike in other liberalised network sectors, the government interfered continually with an incoherent policy, and therefore the industry had no time to establish the favoured structure (Glaister, 2004). There is doubt therefore as to whether the DfT will be any more successful than the SRA in establishing and pushing through a coherent policy.

Furthermore, the government created Network Rail, a private company without private disciplines, seemingly to keep the enormous costs of the railway infrastructure away from its own balance sheet. The decision to place Railtrack in administration, and replace it with a not-for-dividend company, may have weakened incentives for cost control at a critical time for the industry. The ownership structure of Network Rail could be seen as weak because many of its participants are just ordinary people and most (labour unions, the SRA, TOCs) have incentives to argue for more government spending on the railways. With its new powers Network Rail will become the major player within the industry. The DfT will set the policy and Network Rail will implement it. Given that there might be no 'new' binding arrangement, there could, as a result, be no formal link between the government and Network Rail, and therefore weaker rather than stronger accountability.

Like many others, Foster and Castles (2004) see the main problems as being the weak performance improvement since Hatfield and the scale of public resources allocated to rail owing to the alarming increase in industry costs after the Hatfield derailment. The ORR (2004) points out (as stated above) that the government already has the power to determine how much money it puts into the railways. The ORR argues, as well, that there was no legal overlap or conflict concerning the roles and powers of the SRA and the ORR, but there has been some confusion about the behaviour of these institutions. With the abolition of the SRA this problem will no longer exist.

To sum up, the interviews and submissions reveal that most of the problems are of a contractual nature and more related to behaviour and implementation issues than to fundamental structural problems. In the concluding section we summarise which of the main features of the reform of the British rail system worked well and which were problematic.

Rail restructuring – success and failures

Privatisation of the railways differed significantly from privatisation of other network industries in that a franchising system was set up in which the government still had extensive control over passenger services and fares, and provided substantial subsidies to make this possible. In the early years of privatisation, however, traffic growth and cost reductions saw falling subsidies, with some TOCs finding themselves paying a premium to run services.

While there were some difficulties regarding planning, performance and investment, it appeared that the combination of improved contractual relations and the establishment of the SRA was tackling these until the catastrophe of the Hatfield accident. In the aftermath of Hatfield, the government gradually took greater control over the industry, to the extent that all key decisions, including the details of franchising, are settled within the DfT. Arguably this is much greater centralised government control than ever before, even in the days of British Rail. At the same time, there has been an explosion in costs and therefore in government subsidies. To what extent this was necessary as a result of past neglect of the infrastructure is debatable, and it certainly raises again the question of whether a rail network of the current size provides value for money.

In the light of this radical change, it is worth reviewing which features of the privatised railways worked and which did not.

Perhaps the most radical measure in the restructuring of the British rail network was the complete separation of infrastructure from operations. At the time only Sweden had taken this measure, although many other countries have now followed suit.

There is much evidence, and it is widely acknowledged among key people in the industry, that the split of infrastructure from operations is workable. Merkert (2005) reveals that this model works well in Sweden and Richard Bowker, chairman and chief executive of the SRA, said of it: 'I think that the separation of track operations is entirely workable. It is a model that is being rolled out across the whole of Europe. It is actually the fundamental principle around liberalisation and markets. I think it can work, I think it does work and I think it will continue to work better' (House of Commons Transport Committee, 2003). There have been concerns about too much fragmentation of the industry, but these concerns were more about the horizontal than the vertical organisation of the industry. Furthermore, there have been misaligned incentives for both TOCs and Railtrack; until the Periodic Review in 2000 the track access charges were not reflecting all elements of social cost (for example, the scarcity of capacity and congestion) and there were higher transactions costs mainly related to timetabling and maintenance contracts. All these points are of a contractual nature, and not related to the fundamental idea of splitting infrastructure from operations. Foster (2004) argues that if the split has been a problem, it is a very minor one. Moreover the separation has, among other benefits, led to more competition (at least in terms of competition *for* the market, if not competition within the market), more transparency and has been accompanied by substantial growth in traffic on the network.

There is no doubt that the private infrastructure manager, Railtrack, has not worked. The question is whether having a private infrastructure manager was bound to fail, as Wolmar (2001) argues, or whether it could have worked with more careful implementation. It was shown above that Railtrack was badly managed and that most of the contractual environment of this company was weakly designed. Many commentators still favour a private infrastructure manager as it works successfully in other British network industries. Network Rail, the current 'not-for-dividend' infrastructure manager, is formally a private company, but in practice it is able to borrow funds only because it has government backing and is seen as a company that is heavily politically influenced. One could argue that the only reason for its existence is to keep a high-cost utility away from the government balance sheet. Given the ownership structure, which will tend to push Network Rail in the direction of high spending on quality and quantity of infrastructure, much will depend on the effectiveness with which the ORR is able to use its regulatory powers to control Network Rail's costs.

The creation of ROSCOs removed an important barrier to entry in the rail transport market. Nevertheless there were two implementation mistakes in this regard. First, the ROSCOs were initially sold for £1.7 billion by the state, but were subsequently sold on for around £2.7 billion, which represented poor value for the taxpayer (NAO, 1998). Second, there were weak incentives for investment in the early years post-privatisation. Then again the ROSCOs started to invest, and nowadays there is sufficient investment to provide adequate rolling stock of appropriate quality. It is questionable, however, whether there is enough competition among the ROSCOs; arguably greater long-term planning by the franchising body (now the DfT), underwriting longer leasing arrangements, and more efficient allocation of rolling stock would reduce costs.

Open access in freight transport has worked well. Increasing performance and reductions in cost pre-Hatfield are indicators that open access in that market segment is sensible. The small amount of on-track competition in the passenger sector, however, has led to disputes. While it has given rise to lower fares and service innovations, it may lead to duplication of services and inefficient use of scarce infrastructure, as well as, by reducing the revenue of the franchisees, increasing the need for subsidy (Preston et al., 1999).

The question of whether franchising has worked, or not, is an even more complex one. If the objective of the government was to increase passenger traffic on the network, franchising has been very successful, even though much of the change in rail patronage was arguably related to the economic cycle. In the pre-Hatfield period, subsidies were rapidly diminishing, such that in 1999/2000 subsidy per passenger mile had fallen to 3.4p. Many intercity and some London and south-east franchises were operating at a surplus. While there have clearly been some problems with the performance and profitability of the TOCs, most of the problems have arisen because of indecision over refranchising and the disruption following Hatfield. Overall it seems appropriate to regard passenger franchising as a success. In general there appears to be a choice between short franchises, in which public authorities control service planning, fares and investment, and long franchises in which much more responsibility for these is given to the franchisee (Preston et al., 2000). It seems that current policy in Britain lies somewhere between the two, with seven-year franchises, extendable to ten years, close control of services and many fares, but with responsibility for procuring rolling stock resting with the train-operating company.

Regarding independent regulation one could argue that the problems with the infrastructure manager are due in part to regulatory failure. In the early days, the ORR clearly failed to ensure that Railtrack had adequate knowledge of and appropriate investment plans for its assets; although by the time of Hatfield the ORR had taken vigorous action on these issues and improvements were taking place. The ORR has the power to determine the appropriate level of operating and maintenance costs as well as renewal investment requirements, and clearly failed to foresee or control the massive increase in costs in recent years. But perhaps it is unreasonable to expect a regulator to be able to foresee and cope with problems on this scale. Moreover, it is widely agreed that independent regulation is essential to ensure fair access to the network as well as to protect private investment, and the White Paper reasserts the independence of the ORR.

A further highly controversial issue is the case for an organisation such as the Strategic Rail Authority. There is a widespread view that, as originally constituted, the privatised railway lacked leadership in terms of planning and investment. The SRA filled this gap, and some of the arguments of the White Paper for its abolition seem spurious; since the government controlled it and set its objectives, there was no necessary difficulty in its providing leadership to the industry – this should not have led to conflicts with government policy. The SRA's early optimism about the potential for major private investment, however, and indecision on refranchising were already causing problems before the Hatfield accident destroyed its strategy. On the other hand, the SRA has enjoyed subsequent successes in terms of controlling the major West Coast upgrading project, and improving track utilisation. It is not obvious that a government department will perform these functions better.

To sum up, all major characteristics of the rail reform in Britain are seen as workable. While implementation of the reform was rushed and in some respects inadequately thought through, at the time of the Hatfield accident these problems were being tackled, and it is not clear that major structural changes were needed. The outcome of the rail structure review of 2004 in practice leaves most of the structure unchanged, and the one major change – the abolition of the SRA and the transfer of its strategic functions to a government department – is inadequately justified and of doubtful value.

References

Bastow, K. (2004), personal communication.
CfIT (Commission for Integrated Transport) (2001), *Fact Sheet No. 1: The Impact of Post Hatfield Rail Disruption*, available from http://www.cfti.cov.uk/factsheets/01/index.htm, accessed 3 June 2004.
Cowie, J. (2002), 'Subsidy and productivity in the privatised British passenger railway', *Economic Issues*, 7(1): 25–37.

Crompton, G. and R. Jupe (2003), 'A lot of friction at the interfaces: the regulation of Britain's privatised railway system', *Financial Accountability and Management*, 19(4): 397–418.

Cullen, the Rt Hon. Lord (2001), *The Ladbroke Grove Rail Inquiry*, London: HSE.

DETR (Department of the Environment, Transport and the Regions) (1998), *A New Deal for Transport: Better for Everyone*, Cm. 3950, London: HMSO, July.

DETR (2000), *Transport 2010: The 10 Year Plan*, London: TSO, July.

DfT (Department for Transport) (2002), *Transport Statistics Great Britain*, 28th edn, London: TSO.

DfT (2004), *The Future of Rail*, London: TSO.

DTp (Department of Transport) (1992), *New Opportunities for the Railways: The Privatisation of British Rail*, Cm. 2012, London: HMSO.

Evans, A. W. (2000), 'Fatal train accidents on Britain's mainline railways', *Journal of the Royal Statistical Society*, A, 163(1): 99–119.

Evans, A. W. (2004), 'Rail safety and rail privatisation in Britain', Inaugural lecture at Imperial College London, June.

Foster, C. D. (2004), personal communication.

Foster, C. D. (2005), *British Government in Crisis*, Oxford: Hart Publishing.

Foster, C. D. and C. Castles (2004), 'Creating a viable railway for Britain – what has gone wrong and how to fix it', Submission to the 2004 Department for Transport Rail Review, March.

Glaister, S. (2002), 'UK transport policy 1997–2001', *Oxford Review of Economic Policy*, 18(2): 154–86.

Glaister, S. (2004), personal communication.

Goddard, J. (2004), 'Understanding industry costs', Paper presented to the Institute of Economic Affairs' 4th Annual Conference: The Future of UK Rail, London, June.

Grayling, T. (2001), *Getting Back on Track – Reforming the Ownership and Regulation of Britain's Railways*, London: IPPR.

Harris, N. G. and E. Godward (1997), *The Privatisation of British Rail*, London: Railway Consultancy Press/A. & N. Harris.

House of Commons Transport Committee (2003), *Transport – Minutes of Evidence*, Examination of witnesses, Mr Richard Bowker, question nos 1480–1499, November.

House of Commons Transport Committee (2004), 'The future of the railway', *Seventh Report of Session 2003–04*, vol. 1, HC 145–1, London: TSO.

HSE (Health and Safety Executive) (2003a), 'Train derailment at Potters Bar 10 May 2002', Progress report by the HSE Investigation Board, May.

HSE (2003b), *Railway Safety 2002/03*, Sudbury: HSE.

IBM and C. Kirchner (2004), Rail Liberalisation Index 2004, available at www.db.de/site/shared/en/file_attachements/position_papers/study_rail_liberalisation_index_2004_complete_version.pdf, accessed 18 March 2006.

Kain, P. (1998), 'The reform of rail transport in Great Britain', *Journal of Transport Economics and Policy*, 32(2): 247–66.

Kennedy, J. and A. S. J. Smith (2004), 'Assessing the efficient cost of sustaining Britain's rail network: perspectives based on zonal comparisons', *Journal of Transport Economics and Policy*, 38(2): 157–90.

Mercer Management Consulting and DTLR (2002), *The GB Rail Industry: In its own words – problems and solutions*, Report commissioned by the Department for Transport, Local Government and the Regions, London, May.

Merkert, R. (2005), 'Die Liberalisierung des Eisenbahnsektors in Schweden', *Zeitschrift für Verkehrswissenschaft*, 76(2): 134–63.

NAO (National Audit Office) (1998), *Privatisation of the Rolling Stock Leasing Companies*, HC 576, Session 1997–8, London: HMSO.

Nash, C. A. (2002), 'Regulatory reform in rail transport – the UK experience', *Swedish Economic Policy Review*, 9(2): 257–86.

Nash, C. A. (2004), 'What to do about the railways', in C. Robinson (ed.), *Successes and Failures in Regulating and Deregulating Utilities*, London: Institute of Economic Affairs.

ORR (Office of the Rail Regulator) (2000), *The Periodic Review of Railtrack's Access Charges: Final Conclusions*, vol. I, London.

ORR (2004), '2004 DfT rail review', Submission by the Rail Regulator, London.

Pollitt, M. G. and A. S. J. Smith (2002), 'The restructuring and privatisation of British Rail: was it really that bad?', *Fiscal Studies*, 23(4): 463–502.

Preston, J. (1996), 'The economics of British Rail privatisation: an assessment', *Transport Reviews*, 16(1).

Preston, J. (1999), 'Competition in British railways – what have we learned?', Paper presented to the Danish Transport Conference, Aalborg, August.

Preston, J., G. Whelan and M. Wardman (1999), 'An analysis of the potential for on-track competition in the British passenger rail industry', *Journal of Transport Economics and Policy*, 33(1): 77–94.

Preston, J., G. Whelan, C. A. Nash and M. Wardman (2000), 'The franchising of passenger rail services in Britain', *International Review of Applied Economics*, 14(1).

Shaw, J., W. Walton and J. Farrington (2003), 'Assessing the potential for a railway "renaissance" in Great Britain', *Geoforum*, 34: 141–56.

Shaw, N. (2004), personal communication.

Smith, A. S. J. (2006), 'Are Britain's railways costing too much? Perspectives based on TFP comparisons with British Rail; 1963–2002', *Journal of Transport Economics and Policy*, 40(1): 1–44.

SRA (Strategic Rail Authority) (2004a), *National Rail Trends*, Yearbook 2003/04, London.

SRA (2004b), 'SRA: response to Secretary of State for Transport statement: Britain's railway "rehabilitated"', London, July.

Van de Velde, D. M., F. Mizutani, J. Preston and S. Hulten (1998), 'Railway reform and entrepreneurship', Proceedings of the European Transport Conference, Seminar G, London: PTRC.

Welsby, J. and A. Nichols (1999), 'The privatisation of Britain's railways', *Journal of Transport Economics and Policy*, 33(1): 55–76.

Winsor, T. (2004), 'The future of the railway', Sir Robert Reid Memorial Lecture 2004, London: Institute of Logistics and Transport, February.

Wolmar, C. (2001), *How Privatisation Wrecked Britain's Railways*, Bodmin: MPG Books.

4 THE UK RAILWAY: PRIVATISATION, EFFICIENCY AND INTEGRATION
David E. Tyrrall

Introduction

From its inception, the privatisation of the railway probably generated more controversy, more media coverage and more government intervention than all the other privatisations put together. In January 2004, Alistair Darling, Secretary of State for Transport, announced to the press yet another review of the organisation and structure of the UK railway industry. This culminated in a new Railways Act (2005) in April (see Table 3).

The announcement of the review evinced a variety of apparently incompatible responses:

> The rail review has come not a minute too soon.
> David Begg, *Financial Times*, 20 January 2004

> Labour has reversed the privatisation that gave us better, faster, safer trains.
> Michael Gove, *The Times*, 20 January 2004

> ... the joy of any discussion on the railways is that they've been in such a bad way for such a long time that everyone can blame everyone else for everything wrong.
> Simon Hoggart, *Guardian*, 20 January 2004

In the face of such diversity of opinion, this chapter seeks to investigate the outcomes of rail privatisation. The first section outlines the privatisation process and the post-privatisation structure of the industry. This is followed by an examination of the alleged successes and failures of privatisation, a discussion of their causes, and a review of possible futures for the industry.

Privatisation: process and structure

Up to the 1980s, British Railways (BR) had been essentially a 'social railway', with a strong 'culture of the railroad', combining a social or public service interest with an engineering focus on 'running the railway' (Gourvish, 1986: 577; Dent, 1991). During the 1980s and 1990s there was a steady move towards managing BR as a 'business railway' or even a 'profitable business' (Tyrrall and Parker, 2005). BR steadily reduced operating costs so that public subsidy for the railways in the UK ranged from between 0.35 and 0.12 per cent of GDP (BR, various years) by comparison with a European average of 0.52 per cent (Harris and Godward, 1997).

Although BR Board achieved these successes within a vertically integrated railway and with the benefit of a significant level of corporate railway morale (Gourvish, 2002: 374–83), they had apparently demonstrated that under a business approach rail transport could become profitable, and hence privatisable (Tyrrall and Parker, 2005). When privatisation became a serious prospect for the railways, BR Board preferred the retention of a national and vertically integrated industry (Gourvish, 2002: 433), proffering BR plc as the model for privatisation.

Others took a more jaundiced view of the BR approach, arguing that the 'existing culture is more about keeping the trains running than market-oriented thrust' (MacGregor, transport secretary,

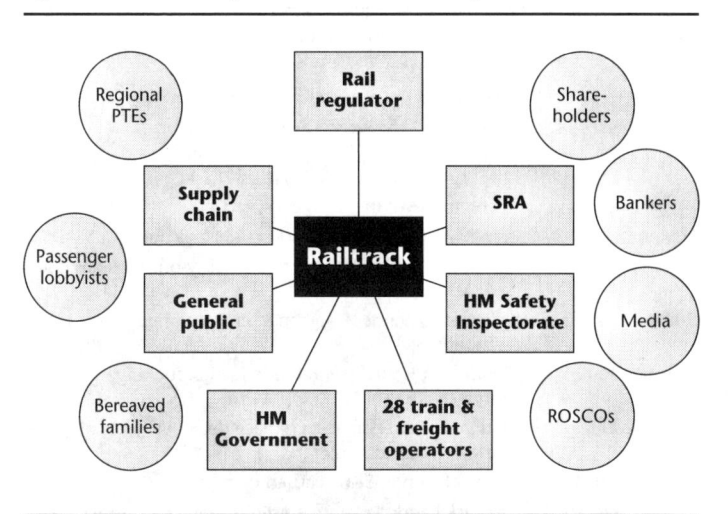

Figure 7   **Rail industry stakeholders in February 2001**

```
                        Rail
     Regional        regulator          Share-
      PTEs                              holders

                Supply                SRA      Bankers
                chain
   Passenger              Railtrack
   lobbyists
                General            HM Safety
                public            Inspectorate    Media

    Bereaved       HM         28 train &
    families    Government      freight        ROSCOs
                               operators
```

introducing rail privatisation, quoted in Murray, 2001: 21). BR command relationships were characterised as 'complicated, inefficient, ineffective and bureaucratic' (Foster, 1994: 7). '[T]he time has come to replace command relationships within British Rail by contractual relationships between free-standing autonomous bodies. The relevant [transaction cost] economics derive from Coase principally through Williamson' (ibid.: 5). In accordance with such principles, the decision was made to split the railway system into around one hundred companies (see Figure 7).

Railtrack, the privatised infrastructure manager, was segregated from 25 train-operating companies (TOCs) and three freight-operating companies (FOCs). The rest of British Rail was divided up to form three rolling-stock leasing companies (ROSCOs) and an extensive supply chain behind Railtrack, including thirteen

Table 3 **Chronology**

1947	UK railways taken into state ownership
1962	Railways consolidated as British Rail
April 1993	Railtrack set up as a division of British Rail
November 1993	Railways Act passed to permit privatisation
April 1997	British Railways Board runs its final train services. TOCs and FOCs take over. Steady rise in passenger and freight kilometres over the following years.
September 1997	Accident at Southall with seven fatalities due to a SPAD
October 1999	Accident at Ladbroke Grove with thirty-one fatalities due to SPAD
2000	Office of Passenger Rail Franchising renamed Strategic Rail Authority (SRA)
October 2000	Accident at Hatfield with four fatalities due to gauge corner cracking
Winter 2000/01	National recovery plan to replace defective rails. Extensive line speed restrictions.
February 2001	Train collision at Selby caused by road vehicle
7/8 October 2001	Railtrack handed over to administrators, Ernst & Young. Railtrack shares suspended at £2.80.
2002	SRA announce consolidation of franchises
October 2002	Network Rail, a not-for-profit company backed by government guarantee, takes over infrastructure from Railtrack
October 2003	Network Rail begins to move infrastructure maintenance in house
December 2003	Winsor, ORR, awards increased maintenance funds to Network Rail
January 2004	Government announces new review of railway structure
July 2004	Government White Paper: *The Future of Rail*
November 2004	Train collision with seven fatalities at Ufton Nervet, near Reading, caused by road vehicle
April 2005	Railways Act abolishes SRA
July 2005	NR and Balfour Beatty employees cleared of corporate manslaughter charges relating to Hatfield accident
October 2005	NR (£3.5m) and Balfour Beatty (£10m) fined for safety negligence at Hatfield. Railtrack Share-holders Action Group loses claim for compensation.

infrastructure service companies (ISCOs) and other support organisations (Tyrrall, 2003). The Office of Passenger Rail Franchising (OPRAF) was set up to sell off franchises to TOCs, while the Office of the Rail Regulator (ORR) was set up to regulate Railtrack, the monopoly supplier of infrastructure. Markets, contracts and regulation would replace administrative fiat as the means of controlling railway activities. This arrangement was admittedly organisationally more complex, but the doctrine that the private sector would provide a better service went relatively unchallenged (Asteris, 1994; Harris and Godward, 1997). With the right contractual system in place, there would be 'a common realisation that all parties will gain more from their joint success than from failure' (Foster, 1994: 8). Furthermore there was widespread agreement that 'separation from Government would free the railways from borrowing restrictions imposed by the Treasury' (Asteris, 1994; Harris and Godward, 1997: 61).

At first, the newly privatised railway prospered, but a series of railway accidents and funding crises led to the demise of Railtrack, its replacement by Network Rail and increasing governmental intervention (see Table 3). In assessing railway performance, critics such as David Hare (2003) catalogue more accidents, worse service and higher costs as symptoms of a malaise caused at least by the complex form of privatisation, and perhaps even by the fact of privatisation itself. On the other hand, advocates such as Gove (2004) point to increased usage, new trains and even reduced costs.

The successes and failures of privatisation

Railway tragedies feature prominently in discussions of railway

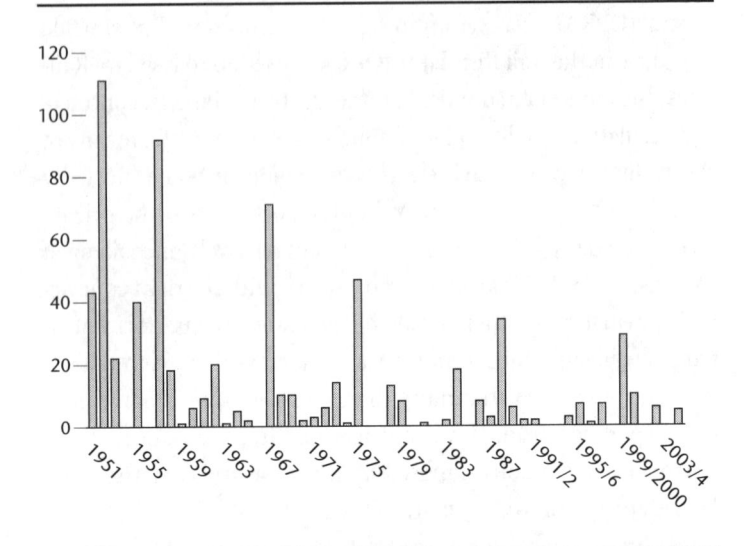

Figure 8 **UK railway passenger fatalities**
1951–2004

[Bar chart showing UK railway passenger fatalities from 1951 to 2003/4, with notable peaks around 1951 (~110), 1955 (~90), 1967 (~70), 1975 (~48), and 1987 (~35).]

performance. Four major accidents occurred during Railtrack's jurisdiction over the infrastructure and a fifth while Railtrack was under receivership (see Table 3 and Figure 8).

Under the nationalised railway, BR had overall responsibility for safety, a role taken over by Railtrack after privatisation (Wolmar, 2001). It has been argued that privatisation had a deleterious effect upon safety on the railways, and that BR, before privatisation, 'generally had in place the best safety systems technically available at the time' (Murray, 2001: 57). Certainly, the accident record since privatisation contrasts unfavourably with the record under BR after Clapham Junction (1988), but not by comparison with a longer history of UK rail accidents (see Figure 8).

No one wants railway accidents, but unfortunately they happen. Since 1951 major UK railway accidents have occurred approximately every nine years, but as railway technology has improved, the trend in the seriousness of accidents, in terms of number of passenger fatalities, has been consistently downward. The period since privatisation has been no exception, with the result that railways remain one of the safest forms of transport (SRA, 2003b).

There has been a substantial increase in the volume of service provided by the railway since privatisation, with both passenger miles and passenger revenues up by over 40 per cent since 1995 (SRA, 2004b, 2005b; ORR, 2005b). This increase has largely been attributed to growth in the economy (Preston and Root, 1999) and increasing road congestion. These would have increased demand regardless of privatisation, but there is no doubt that more imaginative approaches to pricing and promotion since privatisation also played a part (Pollitt and Smith, 2002; SRA, 2003b). The increase in passenger miles was accommodated partly through an increase of at least 20 per cent in train services (train miles) provided up to 2005 (Darling, 2004; SRA, 2004b, 2005b; ORR, 2005b). Increased overcrowding, however, which is clearly a deterioration in quality, has been the other accommodating factor.

Published measures of punctuality and reliability have been changed since privatisation, a point that may in itself be suggestive of deterioration in quality of performance. Pollitt and Smith (2002) point to a slight improvement in these measures prior to Hatfield as indicating a real success when taken together with the marked increase in passenger miles. Success or not, the record immediately after Hatfield (see Table 3) slumped dramatically to around 64 per cent. It has been slowly improving since then towards 85 per cent (SRA, 2004b; NR, 2003, 2005a), but is not currently targeted to reach the 90 per cent levels achieved under BR until 2008/09 (NR, 2005a), although there is some evidence that progress may be faster than this (ORR, 2005b).

The proximate cause of the deterioration in punctuality has been a deterioration in infrastructure quality. Railtrack could and did point, with some justice, to 'decades of state under-investment' (Darling, 2004; Marshall, 2002; Railtrack, 1996/97) and an ageing asset base as sources of the infrastructure problem, but Railtrack were far from blameless. Whereas BR achieved an annual track renewal rate of over 2 per cent of track miles over the whole period 1961–90, this fell to 1.5 per cent during the six years before privatisation, and fell again to approximately 0.5 per cent under Railtrack in the years 1995–2000 (Hope, 2001: 20; NR, 2003). This has risen again under Network Rail to approximately 3 per cent (NR, 2005c).

On the other hand, there has been an increase in the quality of rolling stock (Prideaux, 2004; BBC, 2004), the 'better, faster, safer trains' (Gove, 2004) post-privatisation. The UK now has rather newer trains (average age down from 21 years in 2000/01 to fifteen years in 2004/05; SRA, 2004b, 2005b) with higher speed capability, greater comfort and greater crash-worthiness than under BR. Pendolinos with tilt capability have been introduced. To a large extent, this might have happened anyway. The rolling-stock replacement rate seems to differ little from that achieved under BR, if we exclude the notorious privatisation-induced hiatus in rolling-stock orders in the final years of BR, which served to age the rolling stock handed over to the privatised operators (Gourvish, 2002: 444; Ford, in BBC, 2004). The newer trains have been a mixed blessing. The gradual elimination of slam-door stock reduces passenger accidents but at a cost of longer dwell times in stations and hence slower journeys. This could be mitigated by the speed capability of the new rolling stock, which is under-utilised owing to infrastructure quality, with the overall result that trains 'are generally slower ... and less punctual' (Prideaux, 2004: 44; Ford, 2004) than pre-privatisation. There is some evidence of recent improvements due to timetable alterations, though how far this is indicative of real performance improvement, and how far it is due to alleged manipulation of the timetable measurements, is still to be resolved.

Cost has become a major concern of both the industry and the government. Owing to the fragmented nature of the new railway structure, it is much more difficult to establish the overall costs of the UK's railways than it was under BR (Pollitt and Smith, 2002). Almost all indicators suggest, however, that costs have increased substantially. The cost of BR had been approximately £4 billion per annum, consisting of around £3 billion of passenger and freight revenue and £1 billion of governmental subsidy. It was accepted that after privatisation government subsidy payable to the industry via the TOCs would increase to approximately £1.8 billion per annum initially, but this amount was intended to decline by £200–£300 million per annum thereafter. Early evidence of infrastructure cost savings (ibid.) has either been reversed or may even have been an illusory result of reduced maintenance. It is also becoming apparent that the provision of rolling stock via ROSCOs has increased costs (SRA, 2003a; BBC, 2004), ranging up to 44 per cent return on turnover during their early years (Preston and Root, 1999), including remuneration for alleged risk (Prideaux, 2004). Preston and Root (1999) suggest that about half the increase in subsidy to the industry during the period 1993–97 was due to the increased profitability. In addition, employee costs have increased as unionised, managerial and executive staff have all succeeded in ratcheting up their remuneration. The overall result is that the annual cost of the railways appears to have doubled in nominal terms during the period 1995–2005, with most of the increase being funded via a higher governmental subsidy of over £3 billion per annum (Wolmar, 2001: 244; ORR, 2000; SRA, 2003a, 2004a, 2005a), but also by passenger revenues increasing to over £4 billion per annum (SRA, 2003a, 2005b).

Failures, whether real or apparent, in railway safety, passenger overcrowding and quality have traditionally been matters of government rhetoric but rarely of government action. Cost failures have generally induced government intervention. So it is hardly surprising that cost considerations, especially those arising from the regulator's award of increased maintenance funding to Network Rail in December 2003, led to the January 2004 announcement of another governmental review of the railway organisation in an attempt to identify and reverse the causes of the cost failure.

The causes of cost failure

Transactions costs principles had been applied with apparent success to replace vertical integration with market- and contract-based relationships during other UK privatisations, and were advanced again to support a markets/contracts approach to railway management (Williamson, 1985; Foster, 1994). In the cases of gas, electricity, water, telecommunications and roads, there is a technological argument for this separation. At the very least, the items travelling on these networks do not need timetabling and

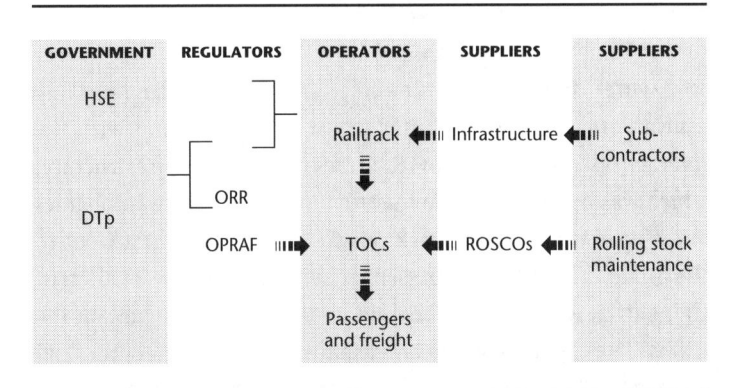

Figure 9 **The 1997 privatised structure: a simplified view**

GOVERNMENT	REGULATORS	OPERATORS	SUPPLIERS	SUPPLIERS
HSE		Railtrack ⬅	Infrastructure ⬅	Sub-contractors
DTp	ORR			
	OPRAF ➡	TOCs ⬅	ROSCOs ⬅	Rolling stock maintenance
		⬇ Passengers and freight		

in all but one case (roads) it is irrelevant if items collide (or even essential that they do). Trains need timetabling to avoid collision, and to optimise network utilisation. Arguably, too, the technology of the moving items and the grid they move on are much more intertwined in the railway industry than in the others cited (ORR, 2002). So it is not surprising that Bitzan (2003) finds economies associated with vertical integration of infrastructure and operations. This is of course the well-known structural argument against splitting track and train.

Commentators, academic (e.g. Gourvish, 2002: 401), railway (SRA, 2004c; Winsor, 2004) and press (e.g. Johnson, 2004: 16), frequently cited the complex structure of the industry in relation to the loss of control, often supporting their argument with complex diagrams with arrows indicating relationships between each of the organisational elements involved (e.g. Figure 7). The joy in such discussion is that connecting lines may be drawn between almost any pair of entities in the railways. Since the number of possible connecting lines (approximately) increases by the square of the number of entities, this makes it quite easy to represent the structure as being very complex indeed.

Figure 9 represents a simplified approach to diagramming railway organisation just after privatisation. Starting with the middle (operators) column, Railtrack owned the infrastructure, which was maintained by infrastructure maintenance companies and subcontractors. Railtrack rented the use of the track out to the TOCs, which carried passengers and freight. The TOCs rent trains from ROSCOs, and maintenance companies maintain the trains. The Health and Safety Executive regulated safety through Railtrack, while the ORR and OPRAF were the conduits for cost regulation of the industry. Interestingly, Armitt (2004) uses a similarly simplified diagram to illustrate the basic flow of money – into the coffers of Network Rail.

Since privatisation, some simplification and consolidation has taken place in the centre and on the right-hand side of the diagram. After the Hatfield accident and the subsequent rapid increase in maintenance spend, Railtrack was placed or forced into receivership in 2001. Railtrack shareholders challenged this act in the courts but lost their case in 2005. Meanwhile, Network Rail took over the infrastructure from Railtrack and began to vertically integrate back along its supply chain by bringing maintenance in house. OPRAF became the Strategic Rail Authority (SRA) with quasi-ownership of Network Rail and closer control over the TOCs (Cracknell and Gadher, 2004; SRA, 2004a). The extension of the SRA's remit over the whole railway began, however, to muddy the relationships on the left-hand side of the diagram, particularly between the ORR and the SRA. This was only partially clarified by the publication of a concordat (ORR, 2002) between the ORR and the SRA.

Despite this limited simplification, the model is still apparently more complex than the pre-privatisation diagram, which featured one connecting line joining one BR to one government. Internal BR organisation charts during the 1980s, however, particularly the matrix organisation, were far from simple (Foster, 1994; Tyrrall and Parker, 2005), a tradition that seems to live on in Network Rail's latest functionally based and colourful but incomprehensible organigram (NR, 2005b). There were and remain a large number of interconnecting relationships between different aspects of railway operation to be managed. Organigrams of other railways (see, e.g., Sweden, Germany and Japan in Van de Velde, 1999) exhibit similar complexity. The problem may not lie so much in any apparent complexity of the structure or indeed in any split of track and train as in the effects of introducing contractual relationships to the industry.

The creation of new contractual relationships created new contractual risks, which are nevertheless real to the entities experiencing them, and for which they require remuneration. ROSCOs need to make investments in specific rolling stock for leasing to TOCs. Similarly, TOCs need to make firm specific investments in employees' knowledge (for example, an estimated training cost of £25,000 per train driver in 1993; Preston and Root, 1999). These firms take the risk that their investments may not be fully recoverable on termination of the TOC contract, and so must price this risk into their franchise or leasing contracts during pre-contract negotiations. Thus ROSCOs recover the cost of new rolling stock over a period of four to twelve years (BBC, 2004; Prideaux, 2004), a cost that would previously have been spread over the 25–40-year life of the equipment. Empirical investigations in the USA show that firms contracting with each other (for example, collieries and electricity generators) in such situations tend to rely on long-term contracts (20–50 years) or even vertical integration (Tirole, 1992). The UK railway industry operates on five-to-eight-year franchises (SRA, 2002, 2004a). In addition, since agglomeration swiftly took hold among the TOCs so that only four or five firms (Armitt, 2004; Preston and Root, 1999) hold most of the TOC franchises and there are only three ROSCOs, the industry structure provides oligopolistic opportunities to force up returns further.

The incentives within the contracts set up at privatisation have also tended to push costs upwards. Fixed access costs paid to Railtrack and the train leasing charges paid to the ROSCOs represented approximately 60 per cent of TOC operating costs (Preston and Root, 1999; SRA, 2003a), limiting TOCs' opportunities for cost reduction. So increased profit had to come from increasing passenger income. Since the marginal costs of running additional train services were small, the TOCs were incentivised to increase service provision, and hence their call upon the capacity of the infrastructure. At the same time Railtrack received 92 per cent of its total revenue as fixed track access income (ORR, 2005a), which incentivised it to increase profit by reducing maintenance expenditure (Wolmar, 2001) and hence the capacity of the system to handle traffic. Railtrack's maintenance suppliers, the ISCOs, also had fixed-price contracts incentivising them to opportunistically reduce maintenance and cost inputs. They did this, in part, by replacing permanent employees with temporary employees (Murray, 2001), which also had the effect of dissipating railway-specific skills, and in part by neglect leading to the Hatfield accident. The court case over Hatfield found both Railtrack (in the guise of its successor, Network Rail) and its maintenance contractor, Balfour Beatty, guilty of safety breaches and awarded fines totalling £13.5 million. After Hatfield the revealed shortcomings in infrastructure maintenance led to the necessity for much increased subsequent spending to reinstate infrastructure capacity (Kennedy and Smith, 2003).

Nor were the perverse incentives affecting capacity confined to the infrastructure. The ROSCOs too operate under fixed-price contracts in supplying rolling stock to the TOCs, and have been reducing maintenance costs (Prideaux, 2004), leading to allegations (BBC, 2004) that the actual maintenance of rolling stock has deteriorated, and shortages of rolling-stock availability (capacity). Problems such as the under-utilisation of higher-speed trains and the non-utilisation of new London commuter rolling stock may be attributed to a failure in coordination of investment in infrastructure and rolling-stock capacities.

These structural and contractual problems could be overcome, at least in part, by the renegotiation of contracts as they reach renewal (BBC, 2004) or by yardstick competition (i.e. comparing the performance of two or more similar entities, for example TOC versus TOC, ROSCO versus ROSCO, etc.), although the efficacy of yardstick competition is limited if the units compared face different conditions (Tirole, 1992). More problematic has been the combined effect of all these changes upon the culture of the railway, the shared goal that the trains would run.

Tirole (ibid.) points out the efficacy of organisational culture in decision-making. Successful privatisation of any state organisation is likely to entail major changes not only to management and organisational structure, but also to organisational culture (Parker, 1995). Owing to the persistence of organisational culture, however, changes to it are likely to be difficult, requiring multiple changes to different aspects of the organisation, and to entail unforeseen consequences (Tyrrall and Parker, 2005). The introduction of management through contracts introduced an antagonistic rather than a cooperative approach to relationships even under the aegis of BR (Dent, 1991; Tyrrall and Parker, 2005), hence fostering opportunistic behaviour inappropriate to such an industry (Pugh and Tyrrall, 2000). After privatisation this situation has been exacerbated. Relationships have tended towards the conflictual (Murray, 2001; Wolmar, 2001), encouraged by contracts demarcating entities and containing compensation and penalty clauses, which again tends to increase operating costs.

Conclusion and possible futures

The restructuring and privatisation of British Rail were not as bad as the direst commentators suggest – but they were not very good either. In summary:

- Safety performance improved. It would have happened anyway, but it did happen.
- The increase in passenger numbers and services seems more a factor of economic growth and road congestion than of private sector market-oriented thrust, although under a Treasury-guided BR this demand might simply have been priced off the railway, and on to the more dangerous roads.
- The passenger increase was a very mixed blessing to the railway, as it increased wear on the infrastructure at the same time as maintenance input was reduced.
- The net result was a decline in infrastructure quality and a

subsequent decline in both line speed and punctuality, which is only gradually being recovered.
- Rolling-stock quality improved. This might have happened anyway, although it is less clear whether we would now have (under-utilised) tilting trains under a public sector railway.
- The most notable failure is, of course, the cost increase.

The contractual and market structure imposed by administrative fiat introduced new risks and perverse incentives leading to some dissipation in railway-specific skills and a major increase in operating costs out of proportion to any increase in either the quantity or quality of outputs. Former BR managers are wont to lament the current situation: 'Give me the economic boom, with 25% more passengers and today's tripled subsidy and we would have supplied the best gold-plated railway in the world' (Jenkins, 2004). And, of course, they are right – except that the Treasury would never have allowed them the funding to do it. Thus, in one sense, privatisation did not lead to 'a common realisation that all parties [would] gain more from their joint success than from failure' (Foster, 1994: 8). In another sense, this in itself was a success – the private sector has been remarkably more successful in extracting egregious ransom from HM Treasury than the public sector railwaymen of BR were. To a large degree the increased funding has been squandered, but the railway is, in places, a little better.

More important than the funding squandered is the opportunity squandered – the opportunity to discover whether the railway would be better managed in the private or public sectors, or whether it would actually make little difference. The UK railway experiment (Tyrrall, 2003) was actually two experiments at once

– one experiment in changing ownership and another in changing structure. This makes it potentially difficult to assess to what extent the observed effects are due to changes in ownership, and to what extent they are due to changes in structure, particularly with respect to vertical integration. From the foregoing analysis, however, it seems clear that organisation (command and control) is superior to markets and contracts as a mode of railway operation. This is far from a novel observation. It is no accident that railways were and always had been vertically integrated entities (Hoskin and MacVe, 2005; Lazonick, 1991), for that is the market-preferred solution to the provision of railways. As Chris Green, director of Virgin Trains, and formerly of BR InterCity, pointed out, 'the nature of the new structure was not decided by experts working within the industry but by people from outside such as consultants, politicians, and civil servants' (Wolmar, 2001: 75). Thus, because of the double nature of the experiment, and because the particular privatisation plan imposed upon the railway system a form of organisation that the market itself would not have created, it is impossible to assess from the UK railway experience whether nationalised railways are the same, better or worse per se than privatised railways.

The cost increase is likely to be long-term or even permanent, and has already ended the supposedly beneficial 'separation from Government [that] would free the railways from ... the Treasury' (Harris and Godward, 1997: 61) and hence from fluctuations in government policy and funding. The need for clarity, stability and a long-term approach in the railway has been a constant refrain over decades from industry leaders (e.g. Parker, 1980; Reid, 1985; Reid, 1991; Bowker, 2004) and even politicians (Davies, 2005). Arguably, government never provided a stable environment for

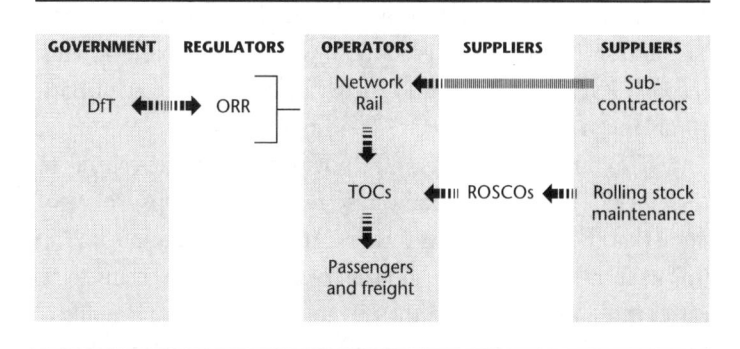

Figure 10 **The proposed privatised structure: a simplified view**

GOVERNMENT	REGULATORS	OPERATORS	SUPPLIERS	SUPPLIERS
DfT ⟷	ORR	Network Rail ⟵		Sub-contractors
		↓		
		TOCs ⟵	ROSCOs ⟵	Rolling stock maintenance
		↓		
		Passengers and freight		

the railway, but at least the changes pre-privatisation could be construed as incrementalism, even if disjointed incrementalism (Gourvish, 2002: 110–11). The UK privatisation, far from being incremental, was 'internationally recognised to be one of the most fundamental changes that have ever been implemented on a national railway company' (Preston and Root, 1999). Perhaps the recent Railways Act (2005) marks a return to incrementalism – in the form of incremental vertical reintegration.

The Railways Act (2005) abolished the SRA and split its tasks between the Department for Transport and Network Rail. This puts the government back in charge of the strategy and the cost of the railways, and of the franchising of TOCs. The HSE will transfer its oversight of safety to the Office of Rail Regulation. Both changes mark a shift to vertical integration on the governmental/regulatory side, but with luck will tend to provide a more stable environment. Network Rail will have wider operational control of the network and is already working more closely with the TOCs, via the establishment of (vertically) Integrated Control

Centres (Cracknell and Gadher, 2004), and by moving TOC and NR management teams into the same buildings (Taylor, 2005). In addition, Network Rail is continuing to vertically integrate up through its supply chain, and there has been a process of horizontal integration among TOCs (Darling, 2005).

These structural matters are not peripheral but central to the efficient running of a railway system, and perhaps we might hope that they will progress further. Actual vertical reintegration (in the form of merging or abolishing organisations) seems to be easier in the public than in the private domain. More simplification has taken place more swiftly on the governmental/regulatory (left-hand) side of Figures 9 and 10 than on the operational/private sector (right-hand) side. Nevertheless, many would argue that Network Rail is de facto, although not de jure, in the public sector. Perhaps the public sector tentacles may further spread into the operational side, thus increasing vertical integration, until we again approach a British/Network Rail structure and hence improve the cost/performance outcomes. Then perhaps we could try a different, but this time controlled, experiment in privatisation – BR plc?

More likely, given that history rarely repeats itself, will be further creeping vertical integration as this is discovered to improve performance and reduce costs. In a review only two years into the UK railway privatisation (1999), Preston and Root concluded that '[f]urther reforms are inevitable' (p. 74). They still are. It is to be hoped, however, that they will be less drastic than those of 1997 or 2001, and maybe even more incremental than those of 2005.

References

Armitt, J. (2004), *The Financing of the Railways*, The Bridge Lecture, London: Network Rail.

Asteris, M. (1994), 'Rail privatisation: a platform for success', *Economic Affairs*, 14(2): 19–23.

BBC (2004), 'Train leasing', *File on 4*, 27 January, www.bbc.co.uk/radio4/news/fileon4/index.shtml.

Begg, D. (2004), 'The rail review has come not a moment too soon', *Financial Times*, 20 January, p. 21.

Bitzan, J. (2003), 'Railroad costs and competition: the implications of introducing competition to railroad networks', *Journal of Transport Economics and Policy*, 37(2): 201–25.

Bowker, R. (2004), Chairman and Chief Executive's Statement, in SRA, 2004a.

BR (1979–1995/96), *Annual Report and Accounts*, London: British Rail.

Cracknell, D. and D. Gadher (2004), 'Regional train czars to cut rail red tape', *Sunday Times*, 18 January, p. 2.

Darling, A. (2004), Statement made by the Transport Secretary to the House of Commons, 19 January, available at www.publications.parliament.uk.

Darling, A. (2005), Speech given to 'The Future of Rail' conference, 3 February, available at www.dft.gov.uk.

Davies, Lord (2005), Opening statement, para. 28, Second Reading of the Railways Bill, available at www.dft.gov.uk.

Dent, J. F. (1991), 'Accounting and organisational cultures: a field study of the emergence of a new organisational reality', *Accounting, Organisations and Society*, 16: 705–32.

Ford, R. (2004), 'Southern power upgrade', *Modern Railways*, February, pp. 56–61.

Foster, C. (1994), *The Economics of Rail Privatisation*, London/Bath: Centre for the Study of Regulated Industries, Chartered Institute of Public Finance and Accountancy, Discussion Paper 7.

Gourvish, T. R. (1986), *British Railways 1948–73 – a Business History*, Cambridge: Cambridge University Press.

Gourvish, T. R. (2002), *British Rail 1974–97 – from Integration to Privatisation*, Oxford: Oxford University Press.

Gove, M. (2004), 'Progress stopped in its tracks', *The Times*, 20 January.

Hare, D. (2003), *The Permanent Way*, London: Faber & Faber.

Harris, N. and E. Godward (1997), *The Privatisation of British Rail*, London: Railway Consultancy Press.

Hoggart, S. (2004), 'Spot the villain in the railways blame game', *Guardian*, 20 January.

Hope, R. (2001), Letter to *Financial Times*, 29 October, p. 20.

Hoskin, K. and R. MacVe (2005), 'The Pennsylvania Railroad, 1849 and the "Invention of Management"', Unpublished conference paper.

Jenkins, S. (2004), 'Track and train must be remarried', *Modern Railways*, March, p. 4.

Johnson, H. (2004) 'Who's who on the railways?', *E-motion*, South West Trains, launch issue, pp. 14–16.

Kennedy J. and A. Smith (2003), 'Assessing the efficient cost of sustaining Britain's rail network', http://ideas.repec.org/p/cam/camdae/0317.html.

Lazonick, W. (1991), *Business Organisation and the Myth of the Market Economy*, Cambridge: Cambridge University Press.

Marshall, S. (2002), 'The UK's railway – the PPP from hell?', Presentation slides displayed by Marshall at the British Academy of Management annual conference, 9 September.

Murray, A. (2001), *Off the Rails*, London: Verso.

NR (Network Rail) (2003), *Business Plan*, available at www.networkrail.co.uk/.

NR (2005a), *Business Plan*.

NR (2005b), *Management Plan*.

NR (2005c), *Annual Report and Accounts*.

ORR (Office of the Rail Regulator) (2000), *The Periodic Review of Railtrack's Access Charges: Final Conclusions*, vol. I, London: ORR, available at www.rail-reg.gov.uk.

ORR (2002), *Developing Better Contract*, Appendix 1, London: ORR.

ORR (2005a), *Access Pricing in the UK*, Presentation.

ORR (2005b), *National Rail Trends, 2005–6, Quarter 1*, available at www.rail-reg.gov.uk.

Parker, D. (1995), 'Privatisation and the internal environment', *International Journal of Public Sector Management*, 8: 44–62.

Parker, P. (1980), Chairman's commentary, British Railways Board, *Annual Report and Accounts, 1980*.

Pollitt, M. and A. Smith (2002), 'The restructuring and privatisation of British Rail: was it really that bad?', *Fiscal Studies*, 23(4): 463–502.

Preston, J. and A. Root (1999), 'Great Britain', ch. 2, in van de Velde (1999).

Prideaux, J. (2004), 'The ROSCOs – the success story of rail privatisation?', *Modern Railways*, February, pp. 44–9.

Pugh, G. and D. Tyrrall (2000), 'Culture, productivity and competitive advantage: the role of consensus in sustaining innovation', *Economic Issues*, 5(3): 5–25.

Railtrack plc (1995/96–2000/01), *Annual Report and Accounts*, London: Railtrack.

Railways Act (2005), available at www.legislation.hmso.gov.uk/acts/acts2005/20050014.htm.

Reid, R. B. (1985), Chairman's statement, British Railways Board, *Annual Report and Accounts, 1984/85*.

Reid, R. B. (1991), Chairman's statement, British Railways Board, *Annual Report and Accounts, 1990/91*.

SRA (Strategic Rail Authority) (2002), *Franchising Policy Statement*, November, available at www.sra.gov.uk.

SRA (2003a), *Strategic Plan*.

SRA (2003b), *Everyone's Railway: The Wider Case for Rail*.

SRA (2003c), *Annual Report 2002–03*.

SRA (2004a), *Annual Report 2003–04*.

SRA (2004b), *National Rail Trends, 2004–5, Quarter 2*.

SRA (2004c), *Corporate Plan, 2004–5*.

SRA (2005a), *Annual Report 2005*.

SRA (2005b) *National Rail Trends, Yearbook 2004–5*.

Taylor, R. (2005), 'Every second counts on UK railways', *Guardian*, 28 October, available at www.guardian.co.uk.

Tirole, J. (1992), *The Theory of Industrial Organisation*, London: MIT Press.

Tyrrall, D. (2003), 'The UK railway industry: a failed experiment in transaction cost economics', *European Business Journal*, 15(1): 38–48.

Tyrrall, D. and D. Parker (2005), 'The fragmentation of a railway: a study of organisational change', *Journal of Management Studies*, 42(3): 507–37.

Van de Velde, D. (ed.) (1999), *Changing Trains*, Aldershot: Ashgate.

Welsby, J. and A. Nichols (1999), 'The privatisation of Britain's railways: an inside view', *Journal of Transport Economics and Policy*, 33(1): 55–76.

Williamson, O. (1985), *The Economic Institutions of Capitalism*, New York: Free Press.

Winsor, T. (2004), 'The future of the railway industry through effective independent regulation', Centre for Regulated Industries Occasional Lecture, 21 January.

Wolmar, C. (2001), *Broken Rails*, London: Aurum Press.

5 ENVIRONMENTALISM, PUBLIC CHOICE AND THE RAILWAYS
Richard Wellings

Introduction

Although accounting for under one tenth of passenger and freight mileage, the railways will receive over one third of the expenditure earmarked in the government's revised 10 Year Transport Plan (see DETR, 2000; DfT, 2004; ORR, 2006: 32–5). It can be argued that rail's prominent role to a significant extent results from the belief among policy-makers that it is a more environmentally acceptable mode of transport than the private motor vehicle. The aim of this chapter is therefore to examine the part played by environmentalism in shaping the government's railway strategy.

It is contended that during the 1990s environmental interests managed to exert significant influence on the transport policy of the UK government. Accordingly, the fuel duty escalator was introduced, the road construction programme was cut dramatically and a new emphasis was placed on supporting public transport. Congestion problems would no longer be solved by expanding the road network. Instead, a combination of incentives and subsidies would be deployed in order to encourage individuals to use public transport rather than private cars.

The change in emphasis began under the Conservative administration in the first half of the 1990s. Apart from an increase in rail subsidies to facilitate the privatisation process, however, spending on public transport was not raised significantly in response to the large cuts in the road programme (DTp, 1997).

The election of a Labour government in 1997 hastened the shift to a 'greener' policy. The Department of Transport was merged with the Department of the Environment in order to ensure that environmental concerns played a more important role in policy development. An integrated transport system was promised in the 1998 White Paper, *A New Deal for Transport: Better for Everyone*, and environmentalism was a key rationale for the measures advocated:

> The effect of noise and pollution is damaging people's health and the quality of life in towns and cities. The countryside is being eroded and we are damaging the wider environment, even changing our planet's climate. A consensus for radical change in transport policy has emerged ... We cannot go on as we were, trying to build more and more new roads to cope with growing levels of traffic. (DETR, 1998: 1)

Although many of the radical measures suggested in the 1998 White Paper were not implemented, in part because of opposition such as the fuel protests of September 2000, environmental objectives have provided part of the justification for recent policy decisions. The government's 10 Year Transport Plan promised to provide a transport system that makes less impact on the environment by 2010 (DETR, 2000: 9), while the 2004 White Paper, *The Future of Transport*, placed particular emphasis on reducing emissions from the transport sector in order to reduce their impact on climate change (DfT, 2004).

Clearly an understanding of the growth of environmentalism in transport policy is essential to any analysis of Britain's railways and their prominence in the government's long-term plans.

This chapter deploys public choice theory in the examination of the political processes that have contributed to the substantial changes in transport policy over the last fifteen years. Following a brief introduction to the main theoretical themes, an account is given of the strategic activities of those special interests heavily involved in the transport field and the extent to which they have been successful in influencing the development of government policy.

Public choice theory

Public choice theory provides insights into the process of policy change by focusing on the incentives facing individual political actors. It is suggested that policy is largely driven by special interests rather than the preferences of the wider general population. This tendency is the result of the logic of collective action. Members of very large 'latent' groups, such as motorists or taxpayers, have little incentive to get involved in political lobbying since the probability of their individual activities making any difference is so tiny (Olson, 1965). It is in their interest to 'free-ride' and let someone else do the work for them, since they will still receive the benefits of successful lobbying for their point of view, whether or not they actually get involved themselves. Thus motorists as a whole benefited from the freeze in fuel duty obtained by the farmers and hauliers engaging in fuel protests, even though they played no significant part in the direct action.

There are three separate factors that keep large dispersed groups from furthering their own interests. The larger the group the smaller is the fraction of the benefit accruing to the whole group that is received by any individual person who joins the action. Second, the larger the group, the lower is the likelihood that any small sub-set of the group or any individual will gain enough from obtaining the benefit to make it worthwhile bearing even a small amount of the burden of trying to obtain the benefit. Third, the larger the group the greater the organisation costs, and thus the higher the hurdle that must be jumped before any gains at all can be obtained (ibid.).

The logic of collective action suggests that, because of the different incentive structures facing individual members, there is a strong tendency for small concentrated interests to be able to exploit large dispersed interests in the extraction of 'rent' from government. Collective action problems make it extremely difficult for large dispersed interests to organise themselves into an effective lobbying organisation. Accordingly, the pattern of special interest action in any field is profoundly influenced by the logic of collective action.

One important tendency is emphasised by Stigler (1971). He suggests that, as a rule, the policy process is acquired by the industry concerned and is designed and operated primarily for its benefit at the expense of the wider public. This tendency reflects the logic of collective action described above. The industry concerned often consists of only a small number of firms whereas the public is representative of a large dispersed 'latent' interest for which the coordination of profitable lobbying activity is virtually impossible.

Industry interests engage in what is termed 'rent-seeking' behaviour, lobbying politicians and bureaucrats to introduce policies that favour their members through contracts, regulations or subsidies. According to Tullock, 'investment in influencing government action appears to have high payoffs' (Tullock,

1989: 4). It might be more profitable for a company to invest a relatively small amount of money in lobbying for policies that suppress competition or increase subsidies rather than investing large capital sums in building new capacity (ibid.). There are, however, large variations from industry to industry in the extent to which company profits are reliant on government policy. These variations create differences in the incentive structures facing companies when they consider the funding of lobbying activities. Accordingly, it would be expected that firms whose profits are heavily dependent on government contracts, subsidies or regulations would exhibit a much higher degree of involvement in lobbying activities than less dependent firms.

While bureaucrats may be one focus of lobbying by companies, they also constitute a special interest in themselves. They have been characterised as self-interested, deploying strategies to achieve a complex set of goals including power, income, prestige and job security (Downs, 1967). If these goals are dependent to a significant extent on the size of the bureaucracy's budget then it will be rational for senior officials to try to maximise the financial resources under their control through a budget-maximisation strategy (Niskanen, 1971). Thus, there can be strong pressure from within government departments to increase expenditure levels. If the welfare of high-ranking civil servants is largely divorced from spending levels, however, it can be rational for them to lobby for the size of their department or agency to be reduced by 'hiving off' low-status responsibilities to other agencies, leaving small, elite, high-status institutions, primarily concerned with policy development (Dunleavy, 1991).

Whether or not the lobbying activities of special interests are successful in changing policy depends in part on the decisions of politicians. It is, however, debatable to what extent their choices are based on the desire to satisfy the preferences of voters. For example, transport policy is just one issue among many, and specific measures can rarely be voted on directly by an electorate. Furthermore, public choice theory suggests that rather than seeking to fulfil the wants of the electorate, both politicians and special interest groups tend to actively attempt to dictate those wants through a process of agenda manipulation (see Riker, 1993). If members of the public desire policy change then, in many instances, the perceived importance or salience of an issue reflects the way in which that issue has been covered in the media. As part of their lobbying activities and rent-seeking behaviour, special interests take advantage of the media's power to persuade by attempting to influence coverage, creating targeted news stories and even trying to control what language is used.

The manipulation of the political agenda by special interests appears to have played an instrumental role in the growth of environmentalism's role in transport policy. The next section therefore identifies the major organisations involved and examines the strategies that were deployed by the lobbyists from the late 1980s to the present day in order to promote a substantial shift in the government's position.

The environmental movement

The shift to a more environmentalist transport policy followed a substantial increase in the salience of green issues in the late 1980s. The membership of both Greenpeace and Friends of the Earth (FoE) more than quadrupled between 1985 and 1989, the year when the Green Party obtained 15 per cent of the vote in the European elections and the combined membership of environmental groups reached 4 million in the UK (Rawcliffe, 1995). Media coverage of the Chernobyl nuclear accident and issues such as acid rain, global warming and ozone depletion had clearly influenced a significant proportion of the population. Indeed, in 1988 Prime Minister Thatcher acknowledged the increasing political importance of environmental concerns, stating, in a well-publicised speech, 'It's we Conservatives who are not merely friends of the Earth – we are its guardians and trustees for generations to come. The core of Tory Philosophy and the case for protecting the environment are the same' (Thatcher, 1988).

Thus, by 1990, boosted by increased memberships and closer contact with ministers and senior bureaucrats, the environmental interest groups were in a far more powerful position than they had been five years earlier. The upper echelons of the Conservative government had also undergone great upheaval with a change in leadership and arguably a shift in emphasis away from free market economic policies. At the same time, the British economy was entering a deep recession and government borrowing was rising at an alarming rate. These particular circumstances provided favourable conditions for special interest groups to intensify their efforts to influence transport policy.

Emissions concerns

The Department of the Environment (DoE) was active in promoting the perception that further government intervention was necessary to reduce the environmental impact of the transport sector. Its 1990 White Paper, *This Common Inheritance*, produced under Chris Patten, identified road transport as a growing source of carbon dioxide and singled it out as a 'sector out of control' (DoE, 1990: 127). The aim of bringing down UK carbon emissions to 1990 levels by 2005 was also stated (ibid.). Meanwhile, the Department of Transport was supervising an acceleration of road construction through the Roads for Prosperity programme. Thus, a conflict of interest between the two bureaucracies appeared to be developing.

Environmentalist interests then made a successful effort to introduce a new dimension to the transport debate: that of urban air pollution. In October 1990 the DoE launched a weather bulletin service that included 'warnings of potentially dangerous air pollution'.[1] Furthermore, when announcing the initiative the DoE spokesman made an implicit link between air pollution and asthma (ibid.). These events received widespread media coverage.

The subject re-emerged in the summer of 1991 after Greenpeace commissioned a study on the effect of air pollution on asthma. According to *The Times*, the report 'concluded there is a definite link between asthma and air pollution'.[2] DoE officials were reported as considering issuing smog alerts, regulations and guidelines under headlines such as 'Pollution takes toll of asthmatics',[3] adding legitimacy to the Greenpeace claims. Friends of the Earth provided an additional report showing 'new medical evidence' on the health effects of exhaust emissions.[4]

Further coverage came in December 1991 with headlines such as 'Health warning as smog covers London' and 'London endures worst pollution'.[5] The apparent source of the information was once

---

1   *Guardian*, 25 October 1990.
2   *The Times*, 24 December 1991.
3   Ibid., 8 September 1991.
4   Ibid.
5   Ibid., 14/15 December 1991.

again the DoE: 'The environment department, which monitors nitrogen dioxide and sulphur dioxide levels, asked the public to restrict its use of cars to reduce exhaust emissions'.[6]

Once ignited, the salience of the air pollution issue rose dramatically, helped by targeted newspaper campaigns such as 'Pollution and the Health of the Nation' in *The Times* and a number of pro-environmentalist BBC documentaries, including Panorama's 'Battling for Air'. By April 1994 a survey by *The Times* revealed that nine out of ten people believed that the government must take urgent action to cut exhaust fumes to protect children from asthma. An ICM poll for the *Guardian*, in August 1995, found a majority of people in favour of banning cars from city centres (Rowell, 1996: 351). Media coverage appeared to have been highly successful at moulding public opinion.

Road protesters

The organised opposition to road construction schemes formed a second strategy in the attempt by environmentalist interests to influence British transport policy. Media interest in the activities of anti-road groups increased significantly following the intervention of the European Community's Environment Commissioner, Carlo Ripa di Meana, in October 1991. The commissioner wrote to the Secretary of State for Transport, Malcolm Rifkind, warning him to block work on a number of construction projects, the most prominent being the M3 extension at Twyford Down. The UK government was accused of breaching European Community directive 85/337 on Environmental Impact Assessments.

---

6   Ibid.

Reports focused on the European dimension until March 1992, when coverage shifted to concentrate on direct action at the Twyford Down construction site by environmental activists. Protesters, said to be members of Friends of the Earth, occupied bridges due for demolition and obstructed contractors' bulldozers. The arrest and jailing of protesters (largely members of the radical group Earth First! (UK)) kept the project in the headlines throughout the summer of 1992.

The manipulation of the transport debate through coverage in the media was clearly a key strategy of the radical environmental groups behind much of the direct action against road schemes. For example, Earth First! (UK) activists staged a number of media 'events' in order to publicise their agenda. These included attempts in the courts to classify a tree house in the path of the Hackney–M11 link road as a legal dwelling, the creation of an 'independent free area', the Republic of Wanstonia, on the same scheme and the unravelling of a life-sized imitation motorway on the roof of the Secretary of State for Transport's house in North London (Wall, 1999: 76–8). Pictures of these eye-catching events often made the front pages of the newspapers, drawing significant attention to both the protesters and their political message (ibid.: 76).

Similar tactics were employed by the larger, more established environmental interest groups such as Friends of the Earth, although their activities tended to be more short-lived given the threat of legal action by the Department of Transport. According to Earth First! (UK) activist Rebecca Lush, Friends of the Earth 'set up this bizarre "we are the middle-class, we are representative of middle England" and extremely media-obsessed camp ... they used symbolism very powerfully, they used the media skilfully and stopped the works with their own tactics' (quoted in ibid.: 68). In fact, because Friends of the Earth played only a limited part in direct, physical attempts to prevent construction at Twyford Down (see Bryant, 1996; Wall, 1999), it might be said that their protest activities were almost entirely aimed at producing media coverage and thereby influencing the transport policy agenda.

The rail lobby

One of the most significant changes to the incentive structures facing transport interests in the last twenty years derived from the gradual commercialisation, then privatisation, of the railways. The private railway industry had been immensely influential prior to World War II. Its strength provides one explanation for Britain's failure to build a road network comparable with those of its major economic competitors during the 1920s and 1930s, another explanation being the relatively strict controls on private motoring (see Plowden, 1971).

The 1990s were a time of great upheaval for the railways. The gradual privatisation of British Rail began in 1994. Before that a long period of gradual commercialisation took place. In 1982, an organisational review divided BR into five sectors: Parcels, Freight, InterCity, Network SouthEast and Regional Railways. Management tasks were reorganised and managers became responsible for specific movements of rail traffic. Accountability of costs and revenue generated by each sector subsequently improved (Nash, 1990: 2). The 1983 Serpell Report found that only 1,630 route miles of the network (about 10 per cent) were profitable (DTp, 1983), although it has been argued that the report took inadequate account of the contributory revenue of supposedly loss-making routes (Henshaw, 1991). Worried about costs, the government gave greater emphasis to the concept of 'a business-led railway'. Under the 'Organisation for Quality' initiative all employees became responsible to a director, who in turn had control over costs and revenue (Hass-Klau, 1998: 7). By the late 1980s the railway had become a largely commercial organisation and Inter-City was able to operate without a direct government subsidy (ibid.). The government began to talk openly about the prospects for privatisation. In 1992 the White Paper *New Opportunities for the Railways* was published (DTp, 1992), outlining plans for franchising services and creating a company responsible for the track and station infrastructure. At this stage a number of private companies began to plan their bids for franchises. Privatisation finally began in April 1994, though it took a further three years to let all the 25 passenger franchises.

After decades of being a loss-making state industry the railways gradually rediscovered the profit motive. This profit was largely artificial, however, in the sense that it was dependent on government subsidy under the Public Service Obligation (PSO). At the same time the viability of the railways was influenced by controls on private road transport. Expensive road fuel prices, inflated by government duty, alter the economics of travel choices in rail's favour.[7] Furthermore, slow and congested roads, as well as strict planning regulations that limit the geographical dispersal of housing and commercial activities, may provide further incentives

---

7 Though the absence of marginal cost pricing, particularly in congested areas, in the case of road transport makes the situation more complex in urban areas – though the congestion that would lead to higher road prices if transport on the current network were priced on an economic basis is partly induced by restrictions on road building.

for using the railways. Thus it would appear logical for a newly commercialised railway to invest in lobbying for policies that would both continue a system of rail subsidies while increasing costs for road users.

Without government intervention it was likely that many rail passenger services, particularly the heavily supported 'Regional Railways' operations, would have had to be withdrawn and many busy commuter routes would have had to charge higher fares. One major caveat is that the railways have long suffered from high levels of bureaucratic inefficiency and expensive safety regulations that bear no rational relation to the relative safety of different transport modes. Thus the network potentially may have been far more viable than it appeared to be. There is also the contested issue of social costs, although high-speed passenger rail may produce externalities equal to or greater than those of road transport (for example, higher overall carbon dioxide emissions per passenger mile).

While many groups associated with railway interests contributed little to the efforts to persuade the government to introduce a more environmentalist policy, Transport 2000 (T2000), a specialist pro-public transport campaigning group founded in 1972, played an instrumental role. From its inception T2000 has had close links with the railway industry. It was formed as the result of a meeting between environmental organisations and railway interests in the context of the leaking of a rail policy review that threatened a massive reduction in the network from 11,600 to 7,000 miles in the interests of commercial viability (Smith, 1995: 98). From the start T2000's most important source of finance was the British Railways Board. Offices and other services were provided by the National Union of Railwaymen

(NUR) (ibid.). In the privatisation era corporate subscribers comprised firms with major stakes in public transport such as National Express, Railtrack, Stagecoach and Virgin Group. Other affiliates include a number of trade unions (including the RMT and Aslef) and several local authorities. Describing T2000 as the 'rail lobby', however, would be rather unfair given the importance of the group's relationships with environmentalist organisations such as Friends of the Earth and bureaucratic interests within government.

Indeed, T2000 staff played an important role in the setting up of ALARM UK, the organisation coordinating the anti-roads protests, and liaised closely with its leaders from more fringe groups (Dudley and Richardson, 2001: 164). T2000 also set up the Transport Round Table, which allowed establishment bodies such as the National Trust, the Countryside Commission and even senior elements of the Department of the Environment to liaise informally with more radical protester groups, such as ALARM UK and Road Alert (ibid.). For example, at a round table meeting on 17 December 1993 discussion ensued on whether any national organisations would be able to help in the training of volunteers for non-violent direct action (ibid.). Thus it could be argued that the radical road protest movement enjoyed significant strategic and logistical support from a number of special interests, including the rail industry (albeit indirectly), established environmental lobby groups and government bureaucrats.

The anti-roads, pro-public transport coalition that had been formed also enjoyed support from within government. For example, T2000 had by the early 1990s fostered close relationships with both the Department of the Environment and the Treasury. The links with the DoE developed after the departure of the economically liberal Nicholas Ridley as secretary of state, when, in part as a result of the 1990 White Paper on *Sustainable Development* and the appointment of the less liberal Chris Patten, the DoE began to take a deeper interest in the environmental implications of transport policy. T2000 was able to help them in relation to their statutory role of commenting on transport schemes.

Elements within the DoE also used anti-roads groups to pass information about Department of Transport (DTp) activities to the press. For example, in 1991 the DTp was planning to abolish grants for rail freight, on the basis of its perception that there were not really any significant environmental costs from road freight. One group heard of the proposal through the DoE and then informed the newspapers. The resulting media criticism resulted in the DTp not only backing away from the abolition proposal but actually expanding the rail freight grant scheme massively. The anti-roads groups also began to brief the DoE about particular road scheme proposals and the department then started to use its statutory powers to prevent certain projects, such as the Hereford bypass, being built.[8]

T2000's relationship with the Treasury during the early 1990s was still closer than that with the DoE. The Treasury, facing a large budget deficit, liaised with T2000's Transport Taxation Group. Accordingly, T2000 was deeply involved in the reining back of the tax refund on company cars in the 1993 Budget. The group was also consulted on the introduction of the steep fuel duty rises in the same year. Perhaps most importantly, T2000 was able to help Treasury officials justify making cuts in the road

---

8   This information was obtained in a taped interview with a senior member of the T2000 staff conducted by the author in November 2002.

programme. Thus the group provided the Treasury with many of the arguments deployed in subsequent public spending round negotiations. Treasury consultations with T2000 on this matter began in 1993, while the major road spending cuts didn't come to fruition until the financial year 1995/96 (the actual decision would have been finalised in late 1994).

Thus by 1994 a powerful coalition had been assembled which sought to bring about change in transport policy. Although the involvement of the Treasury may have been motivated entirely by the need to make spending cuts, environmentalist arguments, implanted in the public's consciousness by a concerted media campaign, provided a useful rationale for a decrease in road expenditure and rises in fuel duty.[9]

The road lobby

The road lobby was in a weak position to resist the shift in policy. The main umbrella organisation for pro-roads bodies, the British Road Federation (BRF), suffered from losses in its membership during the early 1990s and pressure on its budget. In part the decline reflected the depth of the recession, which hit the construction industry (a major component of BRF membership) particularly hard. The organisation also suffered from a form of the 'free rider' problem identified by Olson (1965). A debate started as to whether individual companies should be members or whether their trade association should be. Many companies, particularly in the construction/material supplies sectors, decided to revert to

---

9   Economic arguments were also deployed, emphasising the cost to the economy of congestion. A rise in fuel duty is, however, a very crude method of addressing this problem.

the pre-1960s situation whereby only the trade association would be a BRF member.[10]

The difficulty for the BRF came when these trade associations found themselves in financial difficulty. For example, the British Cement Association scaled back significantly and the Federation of Construction Engineering Companies (FCEC) was dissolved. In a sense, because of the important part the construction industry played in its funding, it can be said that the BRF was somewhat dependent on the road programme for its own financial health. The road programme fed into the profits of the construction industry, which then provided money for the lobby group.

The road lobby also suffered from a weakening of its position within the Department of Transport during the first half of the 1990s. The BRF had for several decades enjoyed a close relationship with the highway engineers of the department (Hamer, 1987). With the formation of the Highways Agency (HA) in April 1994, as part of the Civil Service's Next Steps reform programme, however, the influence of those promoting road building declined within government. The HA, detached from the main department, was unable to defend its budget in public spending round negotiations with the Treasury and had lost one third of its employees by 1997 (weakening the influence of the highway engineers further still). Meanwhile, senior bureaucrats within the core Department of Transport were able to insulate themselves from cuts in the road programme by reorganising and taking advantage of the opportunities for career development presented by both rail privatisation and environmental measures.

A further important element in the decline of the road lobby

---

10 Based on correspondence with a senior official of the BRF.

has been the absence of a powerful motorists' organisation. The AA (Automobile Association) and RAC (Royal Automobile Club) long ago became predominantly commercial organisations providing roadside assistance and politically weak, while newer and more radical organisations, such as the Association of British Drivers, were still in their infancy and did not enjoy much influence within the government or the media.

The lack of a significant motorists' lobby, despite policy changes that have been widely regarded as 'anti-car', appears to be consistent with public choice theories of collective action. In contrast to the rail industry, motorists are a dispersed interest, some 30 million in number. They receive no direct payments from government but are affected by government policy. Their interests are fragmented. For example, urban motorists may hardly feel the effects of fuel duty increases if they generally use their vehicle for short journeys. Other motorists might use public transport to commute to work every day and thus be split as to where their policy interests lie. Motorists are also consumers of public services and taxpayers and thus could take a more general view of high motoring taxes (what they lose in fuel duty they might gain in income tax cuts). Because motorists are a dispersed group, the expected benefit to an individual from political lobbying (such as reduced motoring costs or less congested roads) will tend to outweigh the costs of lobbying. Any costs will be borne by the individual yet the benefits spread widely among a group. This gives rise to the 'free rider' problem and makes effective lobbying much less likely.

Furthermore, the great majority of motorists have faced severe disincentives to engagement in direct action such as that undertaken by the radical environmentalists. In order to run a car, the motorist must have an adequate income or adequate savings. His/her prolonged involvement in direct action could have a deleterious impact on his/her employment. He or she is likely to face high fines and personal assets are at risk from civil action. The motorist is unlikely to qualify for legal aid and may face large legal bills.

But the lack of significant collective action by motorists does not mean that this group is without political influence. The sheer number of motorists and the concomitant potential democratic power should transport become a decisive election issue (even in some marginal constituencies) arguably places significant limits on the degree to which environmentalist demands can be met through policy change.

New Labour and transport policy

The shift to a more environmentalist transport policy continued after Labour displaced the Conservatives as the party of government in May 1997. The new administration immediately imposed a moratorium on road building. The White Paper on integrated transport of August 1998, prepared by the newly merged Department of the Environment, Transport and the Regions (DETR), advocated greater integration between different transport modes, increased use of private finance for public transport and the introduction of local congestion charges with the money raised being spent on public transport schemes.

Although the policy proposals in part reflected the underlying egalitarian ideology shared by socialism and environmentalism (see Wildavsky, 1986), a pronounced increase in the political influence of both the environmental and the public transport lobbies was discernible following the change in government. For example, T2000's access to policy-makers had improved significantly. Indeed, T2000 can be said to have been a major influence on the subsequent Roads Review, which saw almost the entire road programme halted. Accordingly, Deputy Prime Minister John Prescott's major speech on the subject was based on documents prepared by the lobby group.[11] The organisation was also able to float new policy ideas, such as the workplace parking levy and allowing local authorities to tax non-workplace commercial parking, which were then adopted by the DETR. Accordingly, a T2000 insider wrote:

> Transport 2000 is now a central player in preparing this policy and the review of the roads programme associated with it. It is co-organising two private seminars with Ministers to help policy formation on managing demand and reducing car dependence ... and Stephen Joseph [director of T2000] has been appointed to a nine-person expert panel. Assistant director Lynn Sloman has been asked to join a working group on future road safety targets.[12]

On the railways, the government satisfied the preferences of many environmental groups with a pledge to create a Strategic Rail Authority (SRA), designed to bring about a 'railway renaissance', which the government argued had been hindered by the fragmentation of the network caused by privatisation (DETR, 1998). The formation of the SRA went some way towards fulfilling the Labour Party manifesto commitment to increase public control over the industry.

The publication of the 1998 DETR White Paper, however,

---

11 Interview with T2000 official, November 2002.
12 Transport 2000, *Annual Review, 1998/99*.

perhaps represented a peak in the apparent influence of environmental interests over transport policy. The Deputy Prime Minister, responsible for the DETR, was unable to obtain parliamentary time for the 'integrated transport' bills to become law in the 1998/99 session. This suggests that a more environmentalist transport policy was not a key priority at the highest levels in government. Furthermore, strong pressure against some of the more radical proposals in the White Paper had been exerted on ministers by powerful corporate interests, such as the major supermarket chains,[13] which were clearly heavily dependent on private road transport. Another factor in the failure to implement many of the DETR's recommendations may have been a decline in the media coverage of environmental issues compared with the late 1980s and early 1990s.

By the following summer the government appeared to be retreating from the radical policy position set out in the White Paper. It announced that £59 billion was to be spent on roads over the next decade. Although no major new routes were to be completed, apart from the privately funded Birmingham Northern Relief Road, more than one hundred bypasses were to be built and 360 miles of motorway widened. Furthermore, the road planning process was to be cut from an average of ten years to six (DETR, 2000). The 2000 Budget also ended the fuel duty escalator and reduced vehicle excise duty for owners of small cars. The fuel protests of road hauliers and farmers in September 2000 perhaps made it still more difficult for the government to fulfil its original aim of using an array of disincentives for motorists in order to encourage more of them to use

---

13 In a sense supermarket groups are a more concentrated interest group that can lobby on behalf of the dispersed groups of road users.

public transport. Accordingly, the relationship between environmental interest groups and the government deteriorated in the transport field as policy began to depart significantly from environmentalist objectives.

At the same time safety became the overriding priority on the railways, following the Ladbroke Grove crash of October 1999 and the Hatfield crash of October 2000. These incidents produced a very high level of media coverage, most of it highly critical of privatisation, although the number of victims was relatively small compared with the 3,500 fatalities on Britain's roads every year. The Hatfield crash in particular, and the chaos that followed as Railtrack attempted to renew track on large sections of the network, provided an important rationale for the subsequent de facto nationalisation of the infrastructure with the creation of Network Rail in October 2001. Clearly, the short-term aims of improving safety and punctuality now dominated the policy debate rather than any 'rail renaissance' driven by environmental concerns. The government also began to focus on containing growing levels of public expenditure on the railways. Thus, by the time the 2004 White Paper, *The Future of Rail*, had been published, the ambitious targets of the Strategic Rail Authority, to increase passenger traffic by 50 per cent and freight by 80 per cent, by 2010, had effectively been abandoned. Thus there is little chance that the railways will make even a tiny dent in road transport's market share, or, indeed, in the UK's carbon dioxide emissions. It is therefore unsurprising that environmental issues were barely mentioned in *The Future of Rail*.

The importance of environmentalism in British transport policy therefore appears to have declined for the time being. The concerted media-based campaigns of the last twenty years have, however, conditioned the public to the extent that problems such as air pollution provide an easy rationale for future government intervention. Meanwhile, the environmentalist-inspired expansion of the railways under Labour has created powerful commercial incentives for rent-seeking behaviour on the part of the numerous firms now reliant on substantial government subsidies for their profits from the industry. These corporate interests now include a number of multinationals, among them some of the largest banks (for example, through ownership of the rolling-stock leasing companies). It remains to be seen to what extent the rail lobby, reinvigorated by privatisation and high expenditure, will succeed in capturing policy, now that the influence of the environmentalists appears to have waned.

Conclusion

The recent history of British transport policy demonstrates that special interests can have a significant influence on government decision-makers. In the 1990s environmentalist interests were able to take advantage of favourable conditions, such as the high level of government debt and a weakened road lobby, to forge a coalition with bureaucrats from the Department of the Environment and the Treasury, with the aim of undermining the Department of Transport's road programme. A concerted media campaign was launched to influence the policy agenda and persuade the general public of the negative environmental impact of private road transport. The result was a political consensus that further large-scale road building was an unacceptable solution to congestion problems and that the public should be given incentives to use public transport more frequently.

After the election of a Labour government in 1997, the railways were to play an important role in the new strategy. Since road capacity had effectively been capped, railways would have to absorb many of the extra journeys resulting from economic growth in congested areas like the south-east. Despite the ambitions of the Strategic Rail Authority, however, it soon became apparent that increasing capacity on the railways would be extremely expensive for the Treasury (for example, the cost of the West Coast Main Line modernisation has been estimated at £7.6 billion; Hudson, 2004). Thus, it could be argued that concerns over expenditure levels, as well as safety, have gradually replaced environmental imperatives as the key drivers of government decision-making.

Although the extent of their influence has varied over time, the significant role of special interests in the development of transport policy provides a powerful argument against the continued high-level government involvement in the transport sector. The preferences of dispersed consumers and taxpayers may be less important to policy-makers than those of pressure groups, large companies and bureaucrats. Accordingly, it is perhaps unsurprising that there is widespread public dissatisfaction with the quality and cost of Britain's transport infrastructure. Unfortunately, the perceived failure of rail privatisation means that the level of political control over the transport sector is likely to continue to increase in the near future, providing still greater opportunities for special interests to affect policy.

References

Bryant, B. (1996), *Twyford Down: Roads, Campaigning and Environmental Law*, London: E. & F. N. Spon.

DETR (Department of the Environment, Transport and the Regions) (1998), *A New Deal for Transport: Better for Everyone*, London: HMSO.

DETR (2000), *Transport 2010: The 10 Year Plan*, London: TSO.

DfT (Department for Transport) (2004), *The Future of Transport*, London: TSO.

DoE (Department of the Environment) (1990), *This Common Inheritance*, London: HMSO.

Downs, A. (1967), *Inside Bureaucracy*, Boston, MA: Little, Brown.

DTp (Department of Transport) (1983), *Railway Finances: Report of a committee chaired by Sir David Serpell*, London: HMSO.

DTp (1992), *New Opportunities for the Railways: The Privatisation of British Rail*, Cm. 2012, London: HMSO.

DTp (1997), *Transport Statistics Great Britain*, London: HMSO.

Dudley, G. and J. Richardson (2001), *Why Does Policy Change: Lessons from British Transport Policy 1945–99*, London: Routledge.

Dunleavy, P. (1991), *Democracy, Bureaucracy and Public Choice: Economic Explanations in Political Science*, London: Harvester.

Hamer, M. (1987), *Wheels within Wheels: A Study of the Road Lobby*, London: Routledge and Kegan Paul.

Hass-Klau, C. (1998), *Rail Privatisation: Britain and Germany Compared*, London: Anglo-German Foundation for the Study of Industrial Society.

Henshaw, D. (1991), *The Great Railway Conspiracy*, Hawes: Leading Edge.

Hudson, G. (2004), 'The West Coast: in the home straight?', *Modern Railways*, June, pp. 52–4.

Kemp, R. (2004), Presentation to the Institution of Mechanical Engineers, discussed in *Modern Railways*, June, pp. 30–31.

Nash, C. A. (1990), 'Rail privatisation in Britain', *Journal of Transport Economics and Policy*, 27(3): 317–22.

Niskanen, W. (1971), *Bureaucracy and Representative Government*, Chicago, IL: Aldine.

Olson, M. (1965), *The Logic of Collective Action: Public Goods and the Theory of Groups*, Oxford: Oxford University Press.

ORR (Office of Rail Regulation) (2006), *National Rail Trends 2005–2006: Quarter One*, available at www.rail-reg.gov.uk.

Plowden, W. (1971), *The Motor Car and Politics, 1896–1970*, London: Bodley Head.

Rawcliffe, P. (1995), 'Making inroads: transport policy and the British environmental movement', *Environment*, 37(3).

Riker, W. H. (ed.) (1993), *Agenda Formation*, Ann Arbor: University of Michigan Press.

Rowell, A. (1996), *Green Backlash: Global subversion of the environmental movement*, London: Routledge.

Smith, J. H. (1995), 'The politics of environmental conflict: the case of transport in Britain 1972–1992', Unpublished PhD thesis available at University of Cambridge library.

Stigler, G. (1971), 'The theory of economic regulation', *Bell Journal of Economics and Management Science*, 2(3): 17.

Thatcher, M. (1988), Speech to the Conservative Party conference, 14 October, available at www.margaretthatcher.org/speeches/.

Tullock, G. (1989), *The Economics of Special Privilege and Rent-seeking*, Norwell, MA: Kluwer.

Wall, D. (1999), *Earth First! and the Anti-roads Movement*, London: Routledge.

Wildavsky, A. (1986), *The Rise of Radical Egalitarianism*, Washington, DC: AUP.

PART THREE

WHO SHOULD RUN THE RAILWAYS? THE FUTURE OF RAILWAYS AND THE MARKET ECONOMY

6 RAILWAY PRIVATISATION IN THE UK – A LAISSEZ-FAIRE APPROACH TO AN INTERVENTIONIST FAILURE[1]
Oliver Knipping

Politicians and the public alike appear to possess certain fixed ideas about railways that are by no means related to reality. A certain sentimental attraction may be their association with childhood train-sets. Anyone who experienced the floods of quite irrational emotion that accompanied the resistance to close even the least-used lines during the 1960s will be familiar with the problems we face ... (Hibbs, 2000: 47)

Failing state railways

By the 1990s railway systems across Europe had become a heavy burden on public finance and politics. Politicians commonly resorted to the rationale of central planning of railway systems or entire transportation networks, but the results were poor. The centrally planned railway industry in Europe managed to achieve declining market shares in both passenger and freight traffic while being granted substantial subsidies and accumulating debts. Despite protection from competition, the railways failed to compete successfully with other modes of transport.[2]

---

1 This contribution is based on the author's PhD thesis at University College London, 2002: *The Liberalisation of European Railway Markets – Laissez-Faire versus Interventionism.*

2 Knipping (2002: 122–4). Leaving the vast subsidies aside, the railway debt was indeed alarming (figures in billion ecu): Italian railways: 42.1 (1994), German

Since the early days of railways in the UK, politicians and the public had their own ideas of how to run a railway (see the chapters by Hibbs in this volume), whether or not they conflicted with the business perspectives of a profitable railway industry. Though regulation was initially limited, it began in the 1840s and gained pace after the 1870s. Nationalisation schemes in European countries granted exclusive rights to provide public railways or even comprehensive transportation services. In the UK, the 1947 Transport Act nationalised the British railway system and stated as one of the main objectives of the British Transport Commission 'to provide, or secure or promote the provision of, an efficient, adequate, economical and properly integrated system of public inland transport and port facilities within Great Britain for passengers and goods ...'.[3] Whereas politicians and the public proclaimed their concern with regard to the dangers of private monopolies, they were either unaware of the dangers arising from public monopolies or were placing an admirable trust in the workings of public undertakings.

Indeed, the nationalisation of the railway created the only type of monopoly that has insurmountable entry barriers and cannot be challenged by competitors. Governments created legally protected, non-contestable national monopolies and eradicated both actual and potential competition in railway transport or over whole transport markets. In the words of Demsetz, 'The key to monopoly power is the ability of an industry to restrict or retard the expansion and utilization of productive capacity. Government can offer to industry much greater powers of coercion to accom-

---

railways: 33.8 (1993), French railways: 28.7 (1994), British railways: 10.7 (1994), Spanish railways: 8.1 (1994) (European Commission, 1996: Annex I/2).

3   Public General Acts (1947): Transport Act, §3.

plish this end than can be supplied by the industry itself' (Demsetz, 1989: 108). Rather than being disciplined by market forces, state railways were subject to political wisdom, rent-seekers and governments' budgetary constraints. They underestimated the transport market's dynamics and potential, however, as reflected in the loss of market shares despite protectionist efforts.

It is commonly argued that state ownership of railways can be justified on non-economic grounds, such as the achievement of social, environmental, structural and industrial policy goals. While the provision of railway services as a social service produced poor results in terms of quality and value for money, the environmental argument also vanished with highly subsidised and protected railways that were constantly losing market share in freight and passenger traffic. As noted by Nash and Preston, 'the failure of rail companies even to perform well in those sectors in which they have a comparative advantage, such as long distance international passenger and freight traffic, and the perpetual complaints about the price, quality of service and inflexibility of rail transport leads to doubts as to whether railways are currently running efficiently' (Nash and Preston, 1994: 19).

The railways face substantial inter-modal competition in the transport market, having lost market shares in passenger and freight services during recent decades, mostly to road transport.[4] Even though many state railway operators enjoyed exclusive rights on their national rail networks, they still failed to realise that they were acting in the wider transport market rather than in a closed railway market. The railways' power to exploit consumers had been eroded to such an extent that one proclaimed reason for

---

4   Knipping (2002: 123–4, 147 and 197–9 for Europe, Germany and the UK).

nationalisation was the protection of railways.[5] Notwithstanding rail protectionism, public subsidies, regulation of competitors and legally granted national railway monopolies, the situation on European railways steadily deteriorated.

Railway regulation, nationalisation and protectionism dominated the twentieth century. Realising the deteriorating situation of the railways, politicians proclaimed that they would resort to deregulation and privatisation policies in the last decade, which, however, commonly ended up in re-regulation.

Economic arguments for privatisation and deregulation often focus on an increase in economic efficiency and greater independence from politicians. The increased efficiency results from lower costs and the use of economic pricing, together with competitive pressures. The aims of government regarding privatisation are often the raising of revenue from the sale and a reduction of subsidies and deficits (Ewers and Meyer, 1993: 5; Kirzner, 1985: 142).

Government control of the railways was frequently justified by dissatisfaction with market outcomes and so-called 'market imperfections'. The consequence of nationalisation was a monopolised transport industry subject to rent-seekers. Such rent-seeking opportunities may be curbed with privatisation and deregulation policies in open markets (Veljanovski, 1989: 36). The opening up of markets with consequent deregulation and privatisation promotes actual and potential competition in railway markets. The following section analyses the UK's railway privatisation. It concludes that a market-based approach, minimising the potential for even well-intended state guidance and political interventionism, is the way forward, as 'it is quite plau-

---

5 Schmitz (1997: 38) claims that the British railways were nationalised owing to road competition.

sible to believe that government intervention constitutes the main threat to a competitive economy. It is important that this threat be recognized, because our belief on this score governs how we deploy resources to ensure that competition will flourish. What is called for is a redirection of our efforts. Government intervention that has created and sustained monopoly should be our primary target' (Demsetz, 1989: 109).

UK railways between privatisation and re-regulation

During the 1980s the Conservatives' privatisation programme gained momentum with obvious attractions in applying it to British Rail (BR) (Rees, 1994: 45). Government believed that private sector management would bring about more innovation. Also, government would be relieved of its straitjacket relationship with the railways which tied the Exchequer to funding the industry and underwriting its risk (Welsby, 1998: 235–6). Welsby highlights disadvantages of state ownership of the British railways owing to the conflicting aims of railway policy and public policy priorities, while the government had further obligations towards the general economy. 'The result is continuous and inconsistent interference in the management of the company. These conflicts were present for all the old nationalised industries but the temptation to intervene always seemed stronger on the railways than in other sectors. Playing trains has always been seductive for politicians' (ibid.: 236). As a state-owned undertaking, British Rail was largely exempt from the pressures on private entrepreneurs to operate profitably and according to their customers' preferences (Welsby and Nichols, 1999: 57). Nonetheless, British Rail had taken a clear lead role compared with other European railways since the implementation of sector management in 1982. Now the Conservatives wished 'to enable the railways to respond to the increasing demands of customers and to provide the quality of service those customers want' (Freeman, 1992: 82, excluding the original bold print).

Accordingly, the Conservative government's 1992 White Paper, *New Opportunities for the Railways*, proposed a vertical separation between a state-owned national infrastructure company, Railtrack, train-operating companies (TOCs) and freight-operating companies (FOCs). The passenger train companies would own only a few of the assets necessary for their operations. Passenger services were to be organised in 25 temporary franchises, similar to the then profit centres of British Rail.[6] The TOCs would lease their rolling stock from Rolling Stock Leasing Companies (ROSCOs), to which BR's rolling stock was to be transferred prior to privatisation. Railtrack was to provide railway tracks and associated infrastructure, such as electricity supply and the management of depots, stations and the signalling system.

The White Paper proposed setting up Railtrack as a monopolistic state-owned track authority and privatising the freight and parcel operations outright. Temporarily, BR's passenger services would become operating companies under BR's organisation until the entire passenger business had been transferred to private sector franchises. The government envisaged a right of access to the rail network for private passenger or freight operators, so long as they met strict safety and environmental standards, to be overseen by a new regulator (Parliamentary Papers, 1992: 4, 13–14). The fran-

---

[6] Nash and Preston (1994: 24). Initially, the Treasury suggested creating more TOCs, as it anticipated increased competition among the bidders in the franchising process (Shaw, 2001: 9.)

chised passenger services would then compete with open-access train operators on publicly owned infrastructure. Similarly important is the government's long-term objective 'to see the private sector owning as much as possible of the railway. Powers will therefore be taken to allow the future privatisation of all BR track and operations' (ibid.: 4). Also, the White Paper envisaged light regulation for the railways, granting a high degree of managerial freedom to the actors in the new railway market. The ROSCOs and freight operators were to be left almost without regulation and it was assumed that the market would restrain even the TOCs, except for London commuter services. The London area apart, fares policy was to be left to the operators, whereas franchisees would have wide discretion over their output levels, checked solely by minimum service levels that were substantially below the then BR benchmarks. Thus, regulation could largely be restricted to the public sector monopoly in the infrastructure (Welsby, 1998: 236–7).

The 1993 Railways Act, however, considerably watered down the White Paper's proposals regarding open access, the sale of all BR track and operations and light-handed regulation. The minimum service requirements were extended to more restrictive Passenger Service Requirements, and some fares were subjected to regulation. These changes and the open-access provision would have an adverse effect on the franchise bids, owing to potential challenges to the franchisees from open-access operators on their most profitable routes. This naturally reduced the attraction of operating a franchised passenger service and simultaneously increased the subsidy requested in return. Finally, open-access provision was postponed to sweeten the franchises in a package deal of tighter regulation compensated by a temporarily protected industry.

The postponement of open access made the creation of the ROSCOs, which were designed to lower entry barriers, at best redundant. Instead, BR's rolling stock could have been allocated directly to the franchisees. While the idea that leasing companies for rolling stock would facilitate competition in an open railway market owing to a reduction of entry barriers for newcomers was laudable, the logic was eroded in an incontestable railway market. The design of the railway reform provided leasing companies with an income guarantee over many years, as they were sold off after medium-term leases for virtually the entire fleet of rolling stock had been signed. As a result, the TOCs relieved the ROSCOs of the risk of demand variations in the final product market. The regulatory regime applied to Railtrack had a similar effect upon the TOCs, as the Rail Regulator, the sole economic regulator of the railways according to the government's objective, fixed Railtrack's income from access charges in his quinquennial reviews of the pricing regime in 1995 and 2000: they carried only a small amount of variable costs. The TOCs, however, had contractual obligations regarding their output level. The contractual structure discriminated in favour of Railtrack and the ROSCOs, though they rather than the TOCs exhibited market power and were already shielded from competition owing to the regulatory design. Welsby criticises the fact that the TOCs which 'were intended to be the spearhead of commercialism of the railways and the figureheads of the privatised industry' were 'most heavily regulated'. He recommended a reduction in the ROSCOs' market power, a reform of the charging principle in favour of a higher share of variable charges and a reform of the incentive structure in the institutionally separate railway system (ibid.: 9–10).

Though the then Conservative government acknowledged

market power exclusively in the infrastructure and in London commuter services, it pursued a re-regulated railway market predominantly in the area where no considerable market power was assumed, in train operations. Glaister noted this trend: '"administered pricing", "moderation of competition" are being developed as policies which, in the short run at least, are designed to defeat market signals by rendering them irrelevant' (Glaister, 1994: 133).

In their *New Opportunities* White Paper, the Conservatives proclaimed that they would introduce competition and open up the railway industry, moving away from central government planning to control by the market. The Railways Act, however, compromised 'new opportunities' rather than propelling state railways into a free market environment. Nash argues that the design of the system 'left the government with extensive powers over the rail system' (Nash, 2001). Welsby and Nichols add that even though 'the rhetoric of privatisation had been concerned with liberating management, the Railways Act of 1993 had the effect of ensuring that in many ways the privatised industry was subject to more regulation than its nationalised predecessor had ever been' (Welsby and Nichols, 1999: 61). The Office of Passenger Rail Franchising, the public funding body that awarded the franchises to the TOCs and the Rail Regulator, dominated the regulatory framework, complemented by the secretary of state, the Health and Safety Executive and the Office of Fair Trading. Though the Rail Regulator was legally free of political control, as the then Conservative government was concerned about the private sector's willingness to invest in the rail industry, the Office of Passenger Rail Franchising 'was clearly an instrument of government policy, taking its objectives direct from the Secretary of State' (Nash, 2001).

Central planning had, in fact, prevailed over the market, contrary to the government's original objectives. Welsby and Nichols indicate that the privatised industry structure was more tightly regulated than the state-owned BR, and Nash confirms that the 1993 design granted the government extensive regulatory powers over the industry (Welsby and Nichols, 1999: 61; Nash, 2001).

The change of mind was responsible for far-reaching implications in the reform. The incentives of the private rail companies and their actions would have differed markedly if they had had the perspective of full ownership of the temporary franchises at a future date, in addition to harsh competition in the railway market from new entrants, from the very outset of privatisation. Welsby notes that the 'effects of these changes on the smooth operation of the privatised railway were given scant consideration and in some cases it is doubtful if the implications were even understood – for example, the franchised passenger railway finished up with fewer managerial degrees of freedom than were previously enjoyed by BR under state ownership' (Welsby, 1998: 237).

If the 1992 White Paper had, in fact, been enacted, the British approach to privatisation could have been characterised by light-handed regulation. Regulatory forces would have checked the market power assumed in the infrastructure and London commuter operations. Franchised passenger services would have seen minimum service requirements instead of Passenger Service Requirements with an inherent flexibility and with standards developing through a process of competition. The franchised services would have taken care of non-economic services provided for 'social' reasons and received subsidies in return. Open-access operators could have checked the TOC's price/output combination. They might also have challenged claims on subsidised services. The 1992 White Paper advocated choice, which the subsequent reform restricted. Whereas the *New Opportunities* paper suggested that the Conservatives were about to take a European lead in railway reform, releasing British Railways into a competitive market environment, they created an interventionist railway system that was at odds with their earlier propositions in the White Paper. Efforts to deregulate the industry to establish a market for railway services were sacrificed to regulatory interference and ministerial wisdom. In this light it is difficult to award the British model the term privatisation.

Towards a market for railways

In considering future reform we begin by assuming that property rights in the railway industry are clearly distributed, with governments exercising ownership rights and operating railway undertakings. Thus, contractual arrangements between government and potential private railway operators may be negotiated during privatisation proceedings. Those arrangements may include a non-discriminatory open-access provision or obligations to run trains to remote villages with virtually no traffic volume but high costs. Thus all government obligations, compulsory contractual obligations, subsidies, the framework for competition and so on must be established before the privatisation process. If benefits of the market economy are to be reaped, governments must release the industry and refrain from the temptation to exercise overzealous guidance of privatisation processes.

Meticulous planning of privatisation acts against market-based reforms, as the optimal structure of a railway system is unknown (see the chapter by Tyrrall in this volume). Therefore, special effort has to be made to allow the privatised railway system the freedom to adjust according to entrepreneurial potential, market demand, the costs of contracting and the availability of finance without a government straitjacket. Thus, the following proposal is based on the basic insight that scientific predictions in market processes are impossible because knowledge is dispersed across individual members in society. Accordingly, individual planning is superior to central planning.[7] Following the process of releasing the state undertaking into a competitive environment, the most efficient regulation in the railway market is self-regulation through competitive market forces.

Railway services are characterised by the network character of their production. A network is 'a large technical system consisting of different layers of raw services interconnected with each other through which the final consumer service is generated' (Blankart, 1998: 1, without original emphasis). The raw services are interconnected and the capacity of each layer involved determines the capacity of the whole system. Most analyses of railway systems assume a potential for separation into two vertical layers, namely the infrastructure networks and the operation of railway services on the tracks, similar to the vertical separation that had been envisaged for BR.

In the following, three layers of railway services are differentiated.[8] In a simplified version the first layer of railway systems is

---

7   This was the focus of Hayek's 1974 Nobel Prize Memorial Lecture on *The Pretence of Knowledge*; see Hayek (1996: 14, *Die Anmassung von Wissen*). Hall also questioned the basic rationale of planning (Hall, 1969, 1977).

8   Knieps (1996) also proposes to vertically separate railway systems in three layers, rather than two.

Figure 11 **The layers of railway systems**

Layer III	Train-operating companies (carriage of freight and passengers)
Layer II	Network of traffic and safety controls
Layer I	Physical connection of railway tracks

their physical connection, i.e. essentially the railway track infrastructure, with the second layer being a network of traffic control systems, while the train operations comprise the third layer of the system:

Owing to the operation of trains being limited by the maximum capacity the track and the traffic control networks can carry, each layer puts a restraint on the others. Thus, coordination and time-sensitive adjustments between the players in the railway market are essential to produce an efficient railway system. The services involved in the end product require smooth cooperation between all parties. With regard to the final product, 'railway transportation of passengers', it would be useless to offer passengers a seat on a train without the train having the right of way on any track at all. And a railway infrastructure is similarly useless without train operations on its network and a network of traffic signals and safety measures protecting the trains from collisions. The efficiency of the entire network is dependent on efficient production in each layer.

The means of coordination between the layers are, however, controversial, and usually end up in a market versus centrally administered planning debate. Blankart summarises the views of the conventional planning wisdom in noting that the interconnection of the layers can be dealt with 'through either planning or markets, i.e. by hierarchical fiat or by decentralized agreement. According to the conventional wisdom only planning is efficient in a large technical system. Markets would lead to incomplete adjustment in particular in regard to standards ... Note that markets have no role in the conventional wisdom of large technical systems' (ibid.: 2–3).

Market liberalisation acknowledges the dynamism of the railway market, realising that neither the government nor economic wisdom can anticipate future innovations or an efficient market outcome. Instead, it has to evolve by individual action, responding to the individual preferences of actors in the transport market.

In the railway reform proposed here, as many decisions as possible are to be made by market players. The layers will be separated from each other at the outset of the reform, while the layers in themselves will also be split horizontally with various companies initially operating within one layer only. Thus companies would, initially, be able to operate only within one horizontal layer (for example, one train franchise) and one vertical layer (for example, one of layers I, II or III in Figure 11). In order to prevent cross-subsidisation and guarantee non-discriminatory behaviour, no company that operates in any of the layers will be allowed a subsidiary in another layer, as long as public bodies are still involved in the railway market's design. As soon as the privatisation process has been completed and the state's discretionary powers over the industry are withdrawn, the railway industry is then able to respond fully to market forces. Thus, horizontal or vertical mergers and takeovers, joint ventures or other forms of voluntary cooperation are permitted as long as they do not foreclose non-discriminatory open access. Accordingly, inter- and intra-industry concentration is likely to occur over time in order to realise economies of scale or transaction cost reductions, and may lead to market-based integration between train operators and coach firms, airlines, ferry services, taxi companies, road haulage or other companies.

Owing to the absence of sunk costs in passenger and freight transport (layer III), the market for transportation is contestable and subject to both potential and inter-modal competition. This is, admittedly, slightly more difficult in the market for track access (layer I), where sunk costs may lead to what is often considered natural monopolistic behaviour. The initial break-up of the infrastructure will result in privately operated smaller and partly overlaying networks or parallel lines, such as high-speed, regional, freight and mixed-use lines, with different companies operating competing track systems into terminal stations. Having competing track operators serving the same terminal or alternative terminals in an urban conurbation reduces remaining bottlenecks. Owing to competing networks, train operators would route their services over networks according to track access prices, quality of the network, distances and locations. In addition to competition for passenger and freight traffic, however, the track operators are also exposed to constraints such as substitutive competition. Market signals received by train operators would instantly translate into track operators' revenues. Train operators even have a low-cost exit option, not available to track operators owing to sunk costs.

At the core of the railway reform is the intermediate layer of safety operating companies (layer II). Accounting for national characteristics, the safety operators would acquire the signalling and associated infrastructure and take control of safety and traffic management on railway networks as clearing-house institutions for train slots. Concerns about the number of competing track operators would be rendered irrelevant, as their networks and the daily traffic flows of train operators would be coordinated by safety operators.[9] Companies in layer II, however, have no power to exclude or discriminate against train or track operators as long as they comply with pre-defined safety arrangements. Impartial safety operators coordinate orders for train slots through an internal marketplace and guarantee safe traffic planning and daily management. The track operators announce their prices for individual slots to the safety and traffic management company which offers the available slots at prices advertised by track operators without having power over the track companies' access prices or preferences for slot allocation to train-operating companies. Safety operators are in sole charge of the traffic flows and handle potential emergencies within their domain of responsibility directly. Thus, if the company in charge should find a train or track operator offending the rules agreed upon in his safety licence, allocated by a company in layer II, the safety operator may cease all operations on the track in question or those of the train operator involved immediately, until the problems are resolved.

The safety operations can either be organised among a number of companies within layer II, similar to track or transport operators in the other layers, or handled by a single entity. In the case of multiple entities, the safety companies would operate neighbouring networks with the requirement to hand over traffic

---

9 Safety operators would be rather like air traffic controllers in the airline industry, whereas the track operators would be rather like the airport owners.

when it is crossing borders between areas of responsibility.[10] Unlike other aspects of the system, impartial safety management will be operated under long-term government franchises with clear borders of responsibility. Again, a concentration of safety management in the industry may be expected, with operators bidding in several regions or countries during the refranchising process, leading to railway networks that are no longer limited to national boundaries.

In the privatisation as outlined above, private track operators supply the entire track infrastructure of the railway network and compete for traffic volumes with other track providers. They announce (unregulated) prices for individual train slots to the safety operators, who are the clearing-house institutions for train slots and the sole safety regulators of the railway system. Finally, the train operators compete for freight and passenger traffic, ordering the slots from the safety operators and paying prices as announced by the providers of railway tracks, including a mark-up for the services provided by the network safety operators. The safety operators provide an internal marketplace for train slots, while overseeing the safe operations of the railways and non-discriminatory open access as impartial arbiters. Accordingly, the operators of the safety network are at the heart of the railway privatisation proposed here. Following Demsetz's premise that the process of government intervention that created and sustained monopoly ought to be the main target, state

---

10 Technical procedures of traffic hand-over may be undertaken in a way comparable with telecommunication markets, when incumbent operators grant non-discriminatory network access to entrants. Telecommunication operators could emerge as bidders for operators of signalling and safety networks in layer II owing to synergies that include hosting telecommunication networks along the track infrastructure.

intervention is restricted to the provision of a licence to safety operators and general oversight of the competition authority, as in other markets.

References

Blankart, C. B. (1998), *What Can Markets Do in Transport and Telecommunications?*, Paper presented at the 1998 Forum Engelberg: The Future of Mobility and Transport in a Moving World, Engelberg.

Demsetz, H. (1989), *Efficiency, Competition, and Policy. The Organization of Economic Activity*, vol. II, Oxford and New York: Blackwell.

European Commission (1996), *A Strategy for Revitalising the Community's Railways*, White Paper, available at www.europa.eu.int/eur-lex/en.

Ewers, H.-J. and H. Meyer (1993), *Privatisierung und Deregulierung bei den Eisenbahnen – Das Beispiel der Deutschen Bundesbahn und der Deutschen Reichsbahn*, Münster: Institut für Verkehrswissenschaft an der Universität.

Freeman, R. (1992), *The UK Government Perspective*, Presentation at the PTRC Summer Annual Meeting, 14–18 September, University of Manchester.

Glaister, S. (1994), 'The regulation of Britain's privatised railways', in M. E. Beesley (ed.), *Regulating Utilities: The Way Forward*, London: IEA and London Business School, pp. 115–35.

Hall, P. G. (1969), 'Non-plan: an experiment in freedom', *New Society*, 20 March, pp. 435–42.

Hall, P. G. (1977), 'Planning's museum of disasters', *New Society*, 22 September, pp. 593–4.

Hayek, F. A. (1996), 'Die Anmassung von Wissen', Nobel Memorial Prize Lecture, Stockholm, in W. Kerber (ed.), *Die Anmassung von Wissen. Neue Freiburger Studien*, Tübingen: J. C. B. Mohr.

Hibbs, J. (2000), *Transport Policy: The Myth of Integrated Planning*, Hobart Paper 140, London: Institute of Economic Affairs.

Kirzner, I. M. (1985), *Discovery and the Capitalist Process*, Chicago, IL, and London: University of Chicago Press.

Knieps, G. (1996), *Wettbewerb in Netzen. Reformpotentiale in den Sektoren Eisenbahn und Luftverkehr*, Tübingen: J. C. B. Mohr.

Knipping, O. (2002), *The Liberalisation of European Railway Markets – Laissez-faire versus Interventionism*, PhD thesis, University College London.

Nash, C. A. (2001), *Rail Regulation and Competition – Developments in Britain*, Paper presented at the 7th International Conference on Competition and Ownership in Land Passenger Transport, Molde, June.

Nash, C. A. and J. M. Preston (1994), 'Competition in rail transport: a new opportunity for railways?', in *Berichte aus dem Institut für Verkehrswissenschaften an der Universität Münster, Ausgabe Nr. 7, Schwerpunktthema: Reform der Eisenbahnen*, pp. 19–37.

Parliamentary Papers (1992), *New Opportunities for the Railways: The Privatisation of British Railways*, Cm. 2012, July.

Public General Acts (1947), Transport Act, 10, 11 & 12 Geo. 6, vol. II, ch. 49

Rees, R. (1994), 'Economic aspects of privatisation in Britain', in V. Wright (ed.), *Privatisation in Western Europe*, London: Frank Cass, pp. 44–56.

Schmitz, M. (1997), 'Die Privatisierung der Eisenbahnen in Grossbritannien', *Vorträge und Studien aus dem Institut für Verkehrswissenschaften an der Universität Münster*.

Shaw, J. (2001), *The SRA's Refranchising Programme*, London: Transport Salaried Staffs' Association.

Veljanovski, C. (1989), 'Privatisation: monopoly money or competition', in C. Veljanovski (ed.), *Privatisation and Competition. A Market Prospectus*, Hobart Paper 28, London: Institute of Economic Affairs, pp. 26–51.

Welsby, J. (1998), 'What next in UK railways?', in M. E. Beesley (ed.), *Regulating Utilities: Understanding the Issues*, London: IEA and London Business School, pp. 231–59.

Welsby, J. and A. Nichols (1999), 'The privatisation of Britain's railways. An inside view', *Journal of Transport Economics and Policy*, 33(1): 55–76.

7 THE PUBLIC–PRIVATE PARTNERSHIP AND THE GENERAL WELFARE
Rana Roy

Introduction: the decade of experimentation
A public–private partnership

Britain's rail industry has evolved through the decade of experimentation initiated by its restructuring in 1994 to become a public–private partnership, confirming, in the language of the 2004 White Paper, 'rail's status as a public service, specified by Government and delivered by the private sector'.[1] It is the private sector, in one form or another, which delivers the management of the infrastructure, the operation of rail services, the provision of rolling stock, and all manner of ancillary services. But, at the margin, it is the level and mix of public subsidy which determines the level and mix of the industry's output.

Clearly, the result is not a privatisation *sensu stricto*. And if the recent monograph from the Adam Smith Institute (Murray, 2005) is a guide, the verdict of those who advocate a strict privatisation is that 'the present railway industry cannot be called privatized in any meaningful sense'. In this view, the 'present railway industry' is, as it is for advocates of nationalisation, a failure. Thus: 'rail privatization should have provided the nation with benefits ... by allowing the invisible hand of the market to take charge. Instead,

---

1 DfT (2004a). Unless otherwise indicated, all assumptions about current government policy on rail refer back to this document.

a complex and confused regulatory framework placed an invisible foot on the industry's throat, choking off the lifeblood of private sector innovation'.[2]

Success or failure can of course be judged only in relation to defined criteria. This paper will argue that, *if its path of development is as we anticipate it to be,* the public–private partnership is likely to prove more conducive to the general welfare than its available alternatives, in respect of both allocative and productive efficiency, in static and dynamic terms.

As a prelude to the main body of argument, however, and in order to confirm that the object to be interrogated is indeed a stable entity – not a happenstance intrusion that has temporarily interrupted the story of privatisation – it may be useful to reflect briefly on some pertinent facts of the present and immediate past.

Success and failure

Pace Murray (ibid.), Britain's rail industry does not immediately strike the eye of the dispassionate observer as being in a 'sorry state'. Notwithstanding the 'invisible foot on its throat', it has reversed decades of declining demand and market share. Today, it is carrying over 1 billion passenger journeys for the first time since the 1950s. Over the last decade, passenger kilometres and tonne kilometres have grown by around 50 per cent; and both passenger and freight services have not only maintained but also increased somewhat their respective market shares. Britain's is the

---

[2] Murray (2005) acknowledges at the outset that '[m]uch of this paper would not have been possible without Christian Wolmar's survey, *Broken Rails: How Privatisation Wrecked Britain's Railways* ... [a]lthough this paper comes to a different conclusion'. The analysis and prescriptions are indeed different – but not the conclusion that the experiment has failed.

fastest-growing railway in Europe. It has built a new high-speed line, it has renovated its rolling stock, and it is rapidly clearing the backlog of maintenance and renewals bequeathed by its nationalised and privatised predecessors, British Rail and Railtrack.

Per contra, there has been a sharp rise in the overall cost of the railway – reflected in part in an increase in public subsidy from around £1 billion per annum pre-privatisation to over £3.5 billion per annum today. If this increase in cost is the denominator against which the increased output and other improvements are measured, the record of success must be heavily qualified.

But to adopt such a measure would be highly misleading. For the increase in overall cost is largely attributable not to the present public–private partnership but rather to problems in the management of the infrastructure originating in the period of its nationalised and privatised predecessors. In particular:

- The backlog of maintenance and renewals: see the chapter by Tyrall in this monograph.
- The spike in spending on safety following Hatfield – which, as Wolmar (2005) argues, is in part a verdict on Railtrack, its role in the accident 'caused by a broken rail as a result of faulty maintenance procedures ... and the aftermath, when thousands of speed restrictions were imposed unnecessarily across the network because the company did not have the expertise to know whether other parts of the track were also at risk of immediate catastrophic failure'.
- The singular fiasco of the West Coast Main Line project, where the estimated cost rose from £2.3 billion to £13 billion before intervention by government brought it down to its current estimate of £7.6 billion.

The true cost of purchasing the achieved increase in output and other improvements – the denominator against which that achievement is properly measured – is, therefore, considerably less than the overall increase in cost. The performance of the public–private partnership can thus be shown to be more successful than is indicated by data that reflects the legacy of the past.

Re-reading the experiment

The emergence of the public–private partnership can also be seen as a natural result, albeit not the only possible result, of the last decade of experimentation once we cease reading this experiment solely or primarily as a case of privatisation that came to be undermined.

For privatisation was *not* the sole objective of the 1992 White Paper and the 1993 Railways Act. The privatisation of infrastructure was *not* proposed in either document. And privatisation *sensu stricto* – *à la* Murray (2005), freed of regulation and stripped of subsidy – has *never* been put to Parliament or the electorate by any government or opposition party.

Rather, from the chronological record provided in Merkert and Nash in this volume, it is possible to identify seven main steps in the evolution of structure and policy:

1 The original proposal in 1992 to separate services from infrastructure and open up service provision to private sector companies through competitive franchising or open-access arrangements.
2 The subsequent legislation and implementation of that policy in 1993 and 1994, respectively, in a particular form: that is,

the fragmentation of BR into over one hundred companies, all of which were transferred to the private sector, except the infrastructure manager, Railtrack.
3 The separate privatisation of Railtrack in 1996.
4 An incomplete specification of the purpose and extent of future public support: as Welsby (1997) noted at the time, the level of subsidy roughly doubled to around £2 billion per annum, with the expectation that it would decline, but without a clear resolution of the issue.
5 A partial resolution of the issue from 2000 onwards, in the form of an increasing commitment by government to provide continuing public funding over the long term.
6 A partial reversal from 2001 onwards of the privatisation of Railtrack, first by placing it in administration and then by establishing Network Rail as a not-for-profit company.
7 A partial reversal over the last years of the fragmentation of the industry effected in 1994.

In short, the original step 1 has been maintained intact through this process.

Tyrrall is right to note that '[t]he UK rail experiment was actually two experiments at once – one experiment in changing ownership and another in changing structure'. But what should also be noted is the *precedence* of the latter over the former, at least in regard to the privatisation of infrastructure. Perhaps it is time to re-read the UK rail experiment first and foremost as an experiment in how to make vertical separation work in the railways, an experiment conducted in tandem with other member states in the EU, rather than as the last chapter in the UK story of privatisation per se.

UK reform as a part of EU reform

As a matter of fact – and, indeed, partly as a matter of law – the restructuring of the rail industry in this country is part of a continuing process of reform across the EU. The UK, along with Sweden, has been a pioneer in this process; but the process itself is, increasingly, a common venture.

Its two main and enduring constituents – the first embodied in EC Directive 91/440 and its sequels, the second initiated by the European Commission's White Paper of 1998, and both restated in the EC White Paper of 2001 – are:

- the vertical separation of potentially contestable services from the naturally monopolistic infrastructure and the liberalisation of service provision so as to permit scope for competition in rail services and elicit thereby an improvement in productive efficiency in service provision;
- the pricing of rail infrastructure at or close to marginal social cost, as part of a marginal social cost pricing rule for *all* inland transport modes, so as to elicit an allocatively efficient level and mix of output.[3]

And both these constituents are based on robust economic reasoning – indeed, the second is, as Nash and Matthews (2001) note, 'a really quite remarkable and all too rare example of policy makers following the prescriptions of transport economics'.

The UK has advanced some distance along this path of reform

---

3   In assessing the 2001 White Paper, Nash et al. (2004) also identify these same two constituents: in their words, 'increasing competition within rail' and 'promoting socially efficient competition between modes'. They include a third item, 'creation of new rail infrastructure', in which the EC has little role and which may be set aside for the present.

– even if its journey has occasionally taken it along other paths. In so far as we continue along *this* path, learning from experience here and elsewhere, there is good reason to expect a highly welfare-positive outcome.

Separation, liberalisation and competition
The argument restated

Of the first phase of the EU reform process, from the Directive of 1991 to the EC White Paper of 1996, it is true to say that the anticipated benefits from vertical separation were over-stated and the conditions required to make a success of it were under-specified. But the experience gained since then, not least in the UK, can provide the necessary corrective.

The case for vertical separation and liberalisation ought to have been stated, and may now be restated, as follows:

- Hitherto, the rail industry has been treated as a natural monopoly, where one firm can supply the entire output more efficiently than many.
- But argument and evidence suggest that the industry consists of a naturally monopolistic core – the infrastructure of track and off-track lines, signalling and stations – and potentially contestable segments, especially in the operation of passenger and freight services.
- Hence, the vertical separation of services from infrastructure and the liberalisation of service provision to permit scope for competition should generate many of the benefits observable in competitive industries – new entrants introducing new ideas and working practices, increased pressure on

incumbents, a sharper focus on customer needs – and result in improved productive efficiency in service provision.
- But this alone cannot secure productive efficiency in the infrastructure or allocative efficiency in the level and mix of output.

Separation versus fragmentation

Stated thus, the case for reform recognises the enduring characteristics of this industry and the rationale for the historical adoption of vertical integration. It insists that there *is* scope for introducing competition and benefiting from it. But it does not pretend that this reform is equivalent to reversing anti-competitive interventions in competitive industries: barriers against textile imports, the nationalisation of motor manufacturing companies, and so on.

In particular, it recognises that there is a trade-off to be made here. As Armstrong et al. (1994) put it: 'If there are large economies of scope between the vertical related activities, then their combination might be significantly naturally monopolistic even if one of the activities by itself is not. In that case competition is likely to be ineffective or inefficient, in which case ... [vertically integrated monopoly] is the best option.'

And this recognition serves to limit both the selection of what is to be separated and the extent of that separation. Thus, the case for reform does not insist upon separating maintenance from infrastructure management; nor does it forbid coordination between the infrastructure manager and train operators in various technical functions from timetabling to incident recovery. Hence, it is not disturbed by the recent instances of *reintegration* which, in his chapter, Tyrrall rightly notes as significant developments – such as Network Rail's integration of its supply chain or its joint control centres with train operators.

On this reading, the departure in policy announced in *The Future of Rail*[4] has served to separate the European agenda described above – the separation of services from infrastructure *as a means of introducing competition in service provision* – from another, older, home-grown agenda with which it had been conflated: namely, as Tyrrall describes it, the replacement of command-and-control as a modus operandi with contractual relations – and, inevitably, contractual risk – at every possible point, *even in the absence of competition*. Britain has now formally abandoned this specifically British agenda. But it remains committed to, and in the lead in, implementing the European agenda.

Thus, while separation of accounts between infrastructure and services is now legally mandatory, not all member states have implemented a full institutional separation as we have (see Nash et al., 2004: Table 1). While open access for freight services is soon to become legally mandatory, not all member states have experience of it as we do. And while competitive franchising for passenger services is still the exception and not the rule elsewhere, it has long been the rule here.

The evidence to date

It remains to ask: how strongly does the evidence gained from the experience to date support the case for vertical separation, liberalisation and competition?

---

4   See DfT (2004a): in particular, the analysis in ch. 1 and the proposals of ch. 4.

Nash et al. state that the evidence is inconclusive (ibid.: ch. 3). On the one hand, citing NERA (2004), they show that the railways of the EU15 have carried through a significant increase in productive efficiency. This is best reflected in a 12 per cent increase in output (traffic units) achieved at the same time as a 20 per cent reduction in employment over the period 1995–2001.[5] The result compares favourably both with productivity growth in many other sectors and the railways' performance in the previous period. On the other hand, they argue that the available studies do not establish a direct relationship between the level of improvement attained and the extent to which separation, liberalisation and competition have obtained.

This conclusion may be over-cautious. Europe's railways have been working within a legal framework mandating a level of vertical separation and increasing levels of liberalisation and competition. A national rail company that today enjoys a monopoly is well aware that it will lose that monopoly tomorrow. Hence, even in the case of railways that are not yet subject to actual competition, the prospect of competition can be said to be a factor in the recent improvement in performance. Competition, as Schumpeter (1987 [1942]) remarked in another context, 'acts not only when in being but also when it is merely an ever-present threat. It disciplines before it attacks'.

Of course, in the UK, the unit operating costs of the train-operating companies have risen rather than fallen in the post-Hatfield years – over and above the increase in infrastructure costs

---

5 See also NERA (2004: Table 1). The authors note that this reduction reflects in part an outsourcing of various activities – but only a part. Total operating costs (including any payments for outsourced work) also declined slightly so that unit operating cost (cost per traffic unit) fell by 13.3 per cent over this period.

– as is shown in the evidence provided in Nash and Smith (2006, in particular Table 6). But given the uncertainties in estimating the full extent of the increase in rolling stock costs (see ibid.) as well as the nature of the learning curve in the franchising process, it would be premature, to say the least, to attribute this temporary problem to competitive franchising per se.

That said, it is important to distinguish between:

- productive efficiency in static terms – minimising unit costs at any given time, by means of minimising 'X-inefficiency' and arriving at best practice with existing techniques;
- productive efficiency in dynamic terms – the continuing reduction of unit costs over time, by means of innovation, or the application of new and superior techniques.

And it may be argued that the observed increase in productive efficiency reflects only the as yet uncompleted adoption of best practice.

But quite apart from the fact that static efficiency is an important virtue in its own right and that the increased pressure to move to best practice is much to be welcomed, the evidence suggests that there is more to the story. The extent of improvement and the constituents of it – the increasing application of automation to reduce labour costs, the use of new technology to achieve savings in fuel costs – indicate the emergence of a dynamic efficiency.

Against this background, there is no reason to suppose that either the EU or the member states, least of all the UK, will choose to break out of the current legal framework on separation, liberalisation and competition. This constituent of EU reform is therefore likely to be maintained here in the foreseeable future even as it is fully implemented across the rest of the EU.

Rather, what we anticipate in those member states where competition already obtains are policies aimed at promoting *more effective competition* – and, thereby, further improvements in productive efficiency. In particular:

- improved benchmarking to inform decisions on competitive franchising as higher benchmarks are established in practice;
- addressing the problem of oligopoly in the provision of rolling stock, and its cost consequences for rail services, by enlarging the market beyond national limits.

On this last point, Foster and Castles (2004) note 'the increasing concern that competition in the rolling stock market is not effective so that the costs of rolling stock leases are too high and the level of profitability of the three ROSCOs is excessive' – but also that this reflects in part 'the small size of the railway rolling stock market and the fragmentation of rolling stock demand between different national railway systems'. Hence, action at a European level to achieve appropriate standardisation will help to reduce unit costs in rolling-stock production, reducing the cost of the product to service operators.

Privatisation
Competition and privatisation

The liberalisation of service provision mandated in European legislation does not require its privatisation. And so long as *cross-border* competition obtains, benefits from competition may be expected to flow through, in part if not in full, to member states that retain public ownership of their national rail companies. Nor is this outcome predicated on the entry of privatised operators from elsewhere; it will also apply when the new entrants are more efficient nationalised operators than the incumbent. In view of this, the likelihood is that the various member states will continue to exhibit a varying pattern of public and private sector provision of rail services.[6]

Nonetheless, the UK has little reason to regret, let alone reverse, the privatisation of *competitive* rail services. Economic reasoning suggests that competition is likely to yield greater benefits when the pool of potential competitors is enlarged. And the experience to date suggests little to the contrary: as argued earlier, a large part of the failure on the cost front is attributable to the monopoly operator of the infrastructure; and, as noted above, a further part is attributable to the oligopolistic provision of rolling stock. As the cost failures originating upstream are corrected, the benefits of private sector provision of rail services should become more clearly apparent.

Privatisation and natural monopoly

The naturally monopolistic infrastructure of the rail industry is another matter. For whereas 230 years of theory and evidence since Adam Smith's *magnum opus* can be called upon to support the case for competition, and hence for privatisation, in potentially competitive activities, the case for privatising natural monopolies does not enjoy comparable support. Indeed, the most seminal

---

6 On the current pattern, see Nash et al. (2004: Table 1).

defence of private sector monopolistic practice, that provided by Schumpeter (1987 [1942]), relies precisely on the 'ever-present threat' of potential competition – that is to say, it does not apply to natural monopolies. In short, privatisation cannot be a default solution here: it must be assessed anew.

It is therefore unsurprising that EU legislation does not in any way mandate the privatisation of infrastructure and that its further evolution is unlikely to include any such mandate. In most member states, public ownership is likely to be maintained – as it is today (see Nash et al., 2004) – in lieu of a robust alternative. What is at issue in the UK is whether the alternative developed here is indeed robust.

Foster and Castles (2004) are right to insist that the unhappy record of Railtrack – including the 'fatal flaws in the contractual arrangements ... for the maintenance and renewal of infrastructure during the privatisation process' – is not a corollary of the fact of privatisation. They go on to argue that, '[u]ltimately, Network Rail should be returned to the private sector where it can operate under private sector disciplines and incentives'.[7] There are, however, several counter-arguments against recreating a Railtrack plc.

Private sector disciplines and incentives do of course operate in natural monopolies; but they do so in an asymmetric fashion. The incentive provided by the prospect of large rewards for success is not automatically enforced, as it is in the case of actual and potential competition, by the prospect of large penalties for

---

7   It should be noted that they add the caveat: 'this is not practical or desirable until it has established an ability to plan, forecast and control its cost and performance reliably. Until this is done the risks of infrastructure supply cannot now be passed back to the private sector'.

failure. Moreover, it is attended by an unwelcome incentive: the incentive to maximise rent through the exercise of monopoly pricing power.

Hence emerges the justification for regulation that seeks in all cases to establish limits to the exercise of monopoly power – and in some cases, including that of UK rail regulation, to construct artificial penalties for poor performance. But regulatory limits, by limiting rewards, can serve to weaken the monopolist's positive incentive to succeed – and artificial penalties can lead to perverse results, as indeed they did in the case of the UK penalty regime.

Of course, regulation can be refined and relaxed in the attempt to maintain the desired incentives. Thus, Armstrong et al. (1994) highlight the theory of hidden costs: since the regulator can know neither the full range of costs nor the full range of potential cost-reducing effort as well as the regulated firm does, it follows that, for any given *ex ante* regulatory settlement, there is scope for the firm to undertake cost-reducing effort and retain the profit from doing so. As it happens, in the case of Railtrack, the hidden costs were so well hidden that they were hidden from Railtrack itself! In any case, to rely on hidden costs as a means of eliciting cost reduction is to accept permanently sub-optimal efficiency. It excludes the possibility of beginning at best practice in the first year of any given period and obliging the enterprise to seek further profit only through improving upon best practice.

The Network Rail solution

In view of the above, the novel solution developed here – private sector management of the infrastructure on a not-for-profit basis, by a company limited by guarantee, under contract to government, with the specifications of that contract emerging from an iterative process based on the regulator's responsibility for assembling a detailed knowledge of infrastructure costs (see DfT, 2004a: ch. 3) – may well prove to be more successful than its tried-and-tested alternatives.

This solution has some important advantages. Since nothing can be extracted out as dividend, the private sector incentive to extract a rent from pricing power disappears. And while the loss of the private sector incentive to maximise profit through increased efficiency, however weakened it may be, is not an advantage, its exit permits the entry of a new factor: the interest of the *clients*, and especially government, in increased efficiency can now be enforced by the regulator's enhanced knowledge of costs and hence enhanced power to elicit cost-reducing effort.

Hence, there is reason to suppose that productive efficiency in *static* terms will be superior to what could be obtained under conventional privatisation. Nor need it be inferior to what could be obtained under nationalisation. The force of 'government scrutiny and accountability' that supplies the necessary disciplines in nationalised industries, as Foster and Castles (2004) describe it, will continue to operate through the contract between government and Network Rail, mediated through the regulatory process. But, and precisely because of the role of regulation, it will not be able to enforce false economies in costs, by depriving the infrastructure manager of the funds required to carry out the tasks expected of it, as government was wont to do in the days of BR.

What remains in doubt is whether this solution is best able to deliver *dynamic* efficiency. As is argued later, that is likely to require further changes, including especially a sharper definition of the role of government. But since the UK is unlikely to risk sacrificing static efficiency in a repetition of the recent past, the solution is likely to endure, amended with care but not abandoned.

Pricing, investment and the role of public subsidy
The case for marginal social cost pricing

The preceding analysis has shown that the first constituent of the EU reform process – separation, liberalisation and competition, sometimes attended by privatisation – has achieved a measure of success in eliciting productive efficiency in the output of the rail industry. Of far greater consequence, however, is the second constituent of reform, announced in EC (1998): the application of marginal social cost pricing across all inland transport modes. For such a rule would secure not only a maximisation of allocative efficiency in the level and mix of the output of the rail industry and of the larger transport sector – and on a continuing basis to boot. It would also serve to limit the role of government and free the industry to define its own role in response to market signals – and thereby serve to promote a culture of innovation.

The case for marginal social cost pricing was set out at some length in Roy (1998), immediately preceding the Commission's White Paper, and in EC (1998) itself. It was subsequently endorsed by European transport ministers in the statement set out in ECMT (2003), at the conclusion of an extensive programme of research. Suffice it here to state it summarily.

Economic theory states that the general welfare is maximised when each good or service is priced at its marginal social cost. When prices rise above this point or fall below it, the gain to the winner is less than the loss to the rest of society. The sum of welfare is thus reduced. The allocation of resources resulting from such prices – that is, the over-allocation of resources to the under-priced good and their under-allocation to the over-priced good – is therefore inefficient, even if each of the goods in question is produced at minimum feasible cost.

Now a deviation of price from marginal social cost is not in itself a good reason for government to intervene. Relative to the welfare optimum, all real-world markets will fail to some degree – if only because the attainment of this optimum in any one market requires that it be attained simultaneously in all markets. But intervention too can carry foreseeable and unforeseeable costs. Hence, it is only in those cases where markets fail systematically, and to a large degree, that government is best advised to intervene directly. For the rest, competition and competition policy may be relied upon to ensure that the deviation of price from marginal social cost is kept to tolerable limits.

In the transport sector, markets do fail systematically and to a large degree. Two types of market failure obtain, compounding rather than offsetting each other. Thus:

- The relatively high fixed costs of modern transport infrastructure result in the average cost of production being considerably greater than its marginal cost. This is most pronounced in the case of rail. Hence, *ceteris paribus*, rail services would need to be priced far above marginal cost in order to cover the total cost of production – that is, depreciation of past investments, maintenance and operation – whether this total cost is borne by a single, vertically integrated railway or by several separate companies in a de-integrated setting.

- The use of transport infrastructure generates large externalities. These include pollution, accidents and the external costs of congestion imposed by new users on existing users whenever the infrastructure is operating at or above capacity. This is most pronounced in the case of urban road use. Hence, road use would be priced far below its marginal social cost if it were priced only to cover the cost to road authorities of depreciation, maintenance and operation.
- And in so far as the modes of transport are substitutes: *ceteris paribus*, their relative prices would prompt a welfare-reducing substitution between modes, compounding the welfare loss in each.

In order to achieve the welfare optimum, it follows that:
- a subsidy will be required to cover fixed costs so as to reduce the marginal price faced by the user to the marginal social cost imposed by his use – and thus price in welfare-increasing consumption that would otherwise be priced out;
- and a tax will be required to internalise external costs so as to raise the marginal price faced by the user to the marginal social cost imposed by his use – and thus price out welfare-reducing consumption that would otherwise be priced in.[8]

---

8 Arguably, a transfer to cover fixed costs should not be described as a 'subsidy' since what obtains in its absence – prices far above marginal social cost – is best described as an excise tax, as it was described in Hotelling (1938, 1939). And a user charge to internalise external costs should not be described as a 'tax' since what obtains in its absence – prices far below marginal social cost – is indeed a subsidy, as is increasingly recognised not only in economic literature but also in debates on formal classification, such as in OECD (2005). But such controversies need not detain the present discussion.

Progress to date and the evidence on potential gains

In the EU member states, as in all advanced economies, governments have long been cognisant of this double market failure in the transport sector. Consequently, they have intervened in transport markets with a battery of subsidies and taxes in an effort to achieve an approximate degree of correction. But the current battery does not come close to aligning prices to marginal social costs – principally, as a result of the absence of a pricing mechanism to charge users directly for their use of scarce resources in the most dominant transport mode: that of roads. Hence, the need for reform.

So far as rail is concerned, several EU member states, not least the UK, have succeeded in aligning user prices reasonably closely with marginal social costs – partly thanks to European legislation on international traffic but mainly thanks to action by national governments and regulators. In the UK, the evidence assembled by Sansom et al. (2001) shows that, as early as 1998, the ratio of revenues to marginal costs in passenger and freight rail services stood at 0.85 and 1.13, respectively. And given the evolution of passenger and freight prices since 1998, it is reasonable to suppose that the relevant ratio in both cases now stands close to 1.0.[9]

But what the evidence in Sansom et al. (ibid.) also shows is that, in 1998, the ratio of revenues to marginal social costs on Britain's roads was less than 0.5. The price paid by road users remains, on average, far below the marginal social cost they impose. *Relative prices* across the transport sector thus remain seriously distorted, resulting in an under-use of rail services and an over-use of roads.

---

9 To be sure, these results are an average and include over-pricing on some routes and under-pricing on others. But on this count, too, there has been progress since 1998.

The progress achieved to date on rail pricing should not be underestimated. Given that the ratio of marginal costs to average costs for passenger and freight rail is generally found to be in the range of 0.6–0.7[10] – and that pricing to achieve full cost recovery without recourse to subsidy would thus require over-charging rail users by up to 67 per cent[11] – it is apparent that the provision of public subsidy has permitted more efficient price settings than would otherwise have obtained.

What have yet to be achieved are the very large gains available from applying marginal social cost pricing across the transport sector – in particular, per-kilometre charging for the use of roads, differentiated by vehicle type, route and time of day – and applying it *as a rule*. This is the most critical transport-sector reform on the European agenda. And in the wake of the 2004 White Paper on *The Future of Transport*, the UK is in the lead in preparing for it (see DfT 2004b, 2004c).

The modelled results reported for the UK in ECMT (2003)[12] show that the comprehensive application of marginal social cost pricing would deliver an overall increase in welfare of around £11 billion per annum. And its application as a rule would mean that allocative efficiency would be maintained on a continuing basis rather than as the temporary result of a policy decision that could be withdrawn as a matter of discretion. Moreover, a pricing rule designed to maximise welfare rather than revenues would deliver an increase in revenues of around £13 billion per annum (and more, if additional revenues from correcting the under-pricing of parking are included).

---

10 See the evidence presented in Roy (1998) and the econometric studies cited therein, from Caves et al. (1985) to Kessides and Willig (1995).
11 For a fuller statement of the argument, see Roy (1998).
12 See also the summary and explanations provided in Roy (2005).

Now the larger part of the overall welfare gain estimated in ECMT (ibid.) is generated by the pricing of road use. And the broadly comparable results reported in the government's *Feasibility Study of Road Pricing* in 2004[13] – including a welfare gain of around £10 billion per annum and a revenue gain of around £9 billion per annum – are exclusively drawn from road pricing, with other modes being disregarded for the purpose of the study.

Nonetheless, the application of a marginal social cost pricing rule would carry several significant implications for the future of rail. These include:

- a more precise correction of rail pricing on each route rather than the approximate correction on average achieved to date;
- the correction of relative prices in respect of substitute modes – and, with it, changes in the pattern of demand for rail services, in particular an increase in demand for passenger rail services in urban areas;
- the informational base to optimise long-term investment decisions and an enhanced capacity to fund worthwhile investments;
- finally, and in so far as a rule-bound process of allocating public subsidy replaces discretionary intervention by government, an enlarged scope for private sector initiative and innovation.

The first two points follow from the analysis above. The last two merit further attention.

---

13 See DfT (2004c) and the comparison of it with ECMT (2003) provided in Roy (2005).

Efficient pricing and efficient investment

Hitherto, governments have sought to address the underlying problem of market failure in transport at two levels:

- by subsidies and taxes to correct user prices for existing infrastructure;
- by public subsidy for investment in new infrastructure, based on the social return on alternative projects as calculated in cost–benefit analysis, so as to permit a higher level of investment than would obtain if investment decisions were to be based solely on the financial return.

As argued in Roy (2001), and irrespective of any incompleteness in cost–benefit analysis per se, the fact is that the actual record of public investment has not generally been faithful to the results of cost–benefit analysis.

There are exceptions to this record. France long maintained a policy of imposing a common hurdle rate on investments in each mode – a social rate of return of 8 per cent through much of the 1990s – which also served as a trigger: projects that overcame that hurdle would proceed. Nor did this necessarily entail an over-use of public subsidy. Projects that met the financial hurdle rate of the SNCF, or the public, private and mixed (SME) road companies, proceeded without subsidy; and projects that did not were subsidised only to the extent required to bridge the gap between the financial and social return.

The record in the UK is another matter. The hurdle rate applied to public investment, which often matched the rate applying in France and was calculated on much the same basis, did not serve as a trigger. The resulting phenomenon of under-investment has been documented elsewhere. Thus, as is shown in Roy (2005), the UK experienced a more or less unbroken decade-long decline in net public investment from 2 per cent of GDP in 1992/93 to the trough of 0.5 per cent at the end of the decade[14] – which translates into a cumulative shortfall of £65 billion through the decade when compared with a constant investment scenario in which net public investment across all sectors had simply been maintained at 1992/93 levels in real terms (see Roy, 2005: Table 6). Government has recognised the problem – which is why, beginning with the 10 Year Plan announced in 2000, it has sought to raise public investment to 2.25 per cent of GDP.

That said, the problem is not reducible simply to a failure to implement the results of cost–benefit analysis. So long as prices remain uncorrected, with scarce road space made available free at the point of use, investing in capacity to meet the demand arising from such sub-optimal prices must result in a sub-optimal outcome for society. The point has not been lost on society. The outcome has often been a state of paralysis. Investment in additional road space is blocked by the recognition that the demand it seeks to meet is only the outcome of an implicit subsidy to road users. And investment in its alternatives is blocked by the insufficiency in demand arising from the current pattern of prices, in particular the excessively high relative price of rail.

---

14 See Roy (2005: Table 5). The fiscal year 1992/93 is an appropriate date from which to chart the course of public investment since it post-dates the main wave of privatisations but precedes the privatisation of rail. As argued above, there is an enduring economic justification for public subsidy for rail. And given the record of past under-investment, there was no obvious justification for a fall in the real *level* of public investment in rail as distinct from its *share* of overall rail investment.

The application of marginal social cost pricing should serve to overcome this paralysis. Once prices are corrected, the gain in welfare from the provision of additional capacity can be accurately assessed. Nor would there be any rationale to deny supply to the now corrected schedule of demand. Investment can at last be transformed into a normalised, rule-bound process.

Moreover, in so far as the problem of under-investment has stemmed from a pressure on public funds as distinct from economic distortions and their political consequences, the reform of pricing should act to ease that pressure and close the funding gap from two directions. Thus:

- *ceteris paribus*, the more efficient use of existing capacity resulting from the application of marginal social cost pricing will reduce the need to expand capacity;
- the increase in revenues resulting from the same will make it easier to fund capacity expansion where it is needed – and without recourse to general taxation.

To be sure, this favourable outcome belongs not to the immediate future but at the end of the process of reform. The 2004 White Paper nominated 2014 as the earliest date for implementing a comprehensive national road pricing scheme. Starting from where we are today, there are urgent investment needs to be met prior to 2014 and beyond it. These include:

- clearing the backlog of renewals and maintenance resulting from past under-investment;
- expanding capacity in urban rail and other public transport in anticipation of the alteration in demand (and in tandem

with it, in the case of London's congestion charging scheme);
- investing in the technology of road pricing itself.

Nonetheless, the long-term outlook is indeed favourable. Starting from the point of application of the pricing rule, and once the necessary adjustments in capacity have been completed, the need for additional capacity will be less than that which would have obtained otherwise. Future investment can thus be redirected from the expansion of capacity to improvements in service quality and cost-reducing technical innovations. The call on public subsidy will be reduced. And, as reported in ECMT (2003) and Roy (2005), the surplus of revenues over current costs accruing to government from the transport sector will suffice to deliver not only the funds required for worthwhile investments but also the wherewithal for reductions in economically damaging taxes on capital, labour and final consumption outside the transport sector.

Rule-bound public subsidy and private sector initiative

It was argued above that, given the underlying market failure in transport, intervention by government is indeed justified in order to secure allocative efficiency in the level and mix of the sector's output. But it was also argued that this intervention has been seriously flawed both in regard to current output and in regard to investment to service future output.

It is not only that the level and mix of subsidies actually provided have been too inexact to achieve their purpose. It is also that the process of determining subsidy has been largely a matter of discretion. And such discretionary intervention is inherently unpredictable – a major source of uncertainty for individuals and businesses, both within the sector and outside it.

The application of the marginal social cost pricing rule would create therefore an opportunity not only to maximise allocative efficiency but also to transform the process of determining public subsidy into a rule-bound process. Henceforth, the pricing rule would determine the subsidy required to secure welfare-increasing consumption in the use of current and planned infrastructure. With such a rule in place, further discretionary intervention to correct this or that aspect of market outcomes would become redundant, the correction having been supplied, *ex ante*, by the rule itself.

In turn, this limitation of the role of government would greatly enlarge the scope for private sector initiative and innovation. Once the growth of the market resumes its natural course on the basis of corrected prices, both customers and suppliers could signal their needs and offers more clearly. And freed of the need to second-guess government, the industry could concentrate on reading those signals and responding to them effectively.

Such a prospect may appear to be far from the public–private partnership as described in *The Future of Rail*. Here, the role of government begins with the imperative of 'Controlling the budget' (see DfT, 2004a: ch. 3). And the first and last items in the proposed iterative process for purchasing its desired outputs from the industry is government determining the budget for rail and determining the final selection of outputs once the cost of alternative options has been established.

But the appearance is misleading. What *The Future of Rail* describes is the government's proposed procedure for establishing its contract with the industry, not the content of it. It does not specify what it is that guides the government's determination of the budget for rail or its initial selection of possible outputs. What the pricing rule provides, by spelling out the current and future consumption that needs to be purchased, is just that guidance.

Of course, it could be argued that government might choose to rule out any such guidance and rely on its own discretion in determining the budget for rail, roads and all other modes. But such an option is politically unsustainable. It implies that government could permit an objective pricing rule to determine taxes on road and rail use (and relevant subsidies on international rail traffic) while retaining purely discretionary decision-making on subsidies for much of rail traffic and for all road and rail investment. Under these conditions, as was noted in Roy (2001), the revenues from congestion pricing in particular would increasingly be perceived as the outcome of a deliberate under-provision of infrastructure. Anticipating this, government is likely to reform both sides of the equation simultaneously – as indeed it did when legislating to grant local authorities new powers on charging for congestion and workplace parking.

Nor is it necessary to await the full implementation of *The Future of Transport* – to wait until 2014 and beyond – in order to begin implementing *The Future of Rail* in a manner that is conducive to private sector initiative and innovation. All that is required is that the procedure for purchasing outputs as proposed by the government is complemented by a transparent process of modelling the future impact on the rail industry's demand and supply-side conditions of the major relevant step-changes in policy that are currently in preparation.

To put it another way: what is required is that government

signals its commitment to complete its programme of reform and end the age of discretionary intervention. Once the industry is assured that the marginal social cost pricing rule and therewith a rule-bound process for determining public subsidy will indeed be instituted, it can begin to prepare the business case for investing in radical innovations appropriate to the expanded market of the future: innovations in the design of urban rail services, in the application of information technology, in fuel efficiency, in progress towards full automation, and so on.

It was argued at the outset that Murray's (2005) reading of the present state of the industry – of 'a complex and confused regulatory framework' placing 'an invisible foot on the industry's throat, choking off the lifeblood of private sector innovation' – is hyperbole. The industry continues to expand, to improve and to innovate. Nonetheless, it is quite true that simplifying, clarifying and limiting the role of government would serve to enlarge the scope for private sector initiative and innovation.

The point is, however, that it is precisely the development of the public–private partnership along the lines indicated above which offers the best promise of stimulating private sector innovation and promoting dynamic productive efficiency. For it can offer this without requiring society – unreasonably and unrealistically – to sacrifice the static productive efficiency gains facilitated by separation, liberalisation and competition or the allocative efficiency gains that can only be secured by public subsidy.

We conclude therefore that, if its path of development is as we anticipate it to be, the public–private partnership is likely to prove more conducive to the general welfare than its available alternatives.

References

Armstrong, M., S. Cowan and J. Vickers (1994), *Regulatory Reform: Economic Analysis and British Experience*, Cambridge, MA: MIT Press.

Caves, D. N., L. R. Christensen, M. W. Tretheway and R. J. Windle (1985), 'Network effects and the measurement of returns to scale and density for US railroads', in A. Daughety (ed.), *Analytical Studies in Transport Economics*, Cambridge: Cambridge University Press.

DETR (Department of the Environment, Transport and the Regions) (2000), *Transport 2010: The 10 Year Plan*, London: TSO.

DfT (Department for Transport) (2004a), *The Future of Rail*, London: TSO.

DfT (2004b), *The Future of Transport: A network for 2030*, London: TSO.

DfT (2004c), *Feasibility Study of Road Pricing in the UK: A report to the Secretary of State for Transport*, London: DfT.

DTp (Department of Transport) (1992), *New Opportunities for the Railways: The Privatisation of British Rail*, Cm. 2012, London: HMSO.

EC (European Commission) (1996), *A Strategy for Revitalising the Community's Railways*, Brussels: EC.

EC (1998), *Fair Payment for Infrastructure Use: A phased approach to a common transport infrastructure charging framework in the EU*, Brussels: EC.

EC (2001), *Transport Policy for 2010: Time to Decide*, Brussels: EC.

ECMT (European Conference of Ministers of Transport) (2003), *Reforming Transport Taxes*, Paris: OECD Publications.

Foster, C. and C. Castles (2004), 'Creating a viable railway for Britain – what has gone wrong and how to fix it', Submission to the 2004 Department for Transport Rail Review, London.

Hotelling, H. (1938), 'The general welfare in relation to problems of taxation and utility rates', *Econometrica*, 6.

Hotelling, H. (1939), 'The relation of prices to marginal costs in an optimum system', *Econometrica*, 7.

Kessides, I. N. and R. D. Willig (1995), *Restructuring Regulation of the Rail Industry for the Public Interest*, Washington, DC: World Bank.

Murray, I. (2005), *No Way to Run a Railway: Lessons from British Rail Privatization*, London: Adam Smith Research Trust.

Nash, C. and B. Matthews (2001), 'Why reform transport prices? A review of European research', IMPRINT-EUROPE seminar paper, Brussels.

Nash, C., B. Matthews and J. Shires (2004), *The EU Transport Policy White Paper: An assessment of progress*, Leeds/Brussels: ITS/CER.

Nash, C. and A. Smith (2006), 'Passenger rail franchising – British experience', ECMT Workshop on Competitive Tendering for Passenger Rail Services, Paris.

NERA (2004), *Study of the Financing and Public Budget Contributions to Railways*, London.

OECD (Organisation for Economic Cooperation and Development) (2005), *Environmentally Harmful Subsidies: Challenges for Reform*, Paris: OECD Publications.

Roy, R. (1998), *Infrastructure Cost Recovery under Allocatively Efficient Pricing*, Paris: UIC.

Roy, R. (2001), 'Means and ends: cost–benefit assessment and welfare-maximising investment', in *Assessing the Benefits of Transport*, Paris: OECD Publications.

Roy, R. (2005), 'Optimal pricing: the route to a self-funding infrastructure – and more', *Economic Affairs*, 25(1).

Sansom, T., C. Nash, P. Mackie and J. Shires (2001), *Surface Transport Costs and Charges: Great Britain 1998*, Leeds: ITS.

Schumpeter, J. A. (1987 [1942]), *Capitalism, Socialism and Democracy*, London: Unwin.

Welsby, J. K. (1997), *What Next in UK Railways?*, Lectures on Economic Regulation Series VII, London: Institute of Economic Affairs.

Wolmar, C. (2005), 'Forget Byers: the scandal was in the original sell-off', *Guardian*, 16 July.

8 RAIL IN A MARKET ECONOMY
Richard Wellings

Introduction

This chapter examines the economic impact of government intervention on the UK's transport sector. The current situation is compared with what might be expected to occur under the conditions prevalent in a pure market economy, in terms of institutional structures, infrastructure provision and competition between modes. By this method it is hoped that insights can be gained into the endemic deficiencies of both the railway industry and British transport policy in general.

The importance of this exercise rests on the essential role transport plays in facilitating economic activity. In the eighteenth century the development of an extensive and integrated network of toll roads was vital to the progress of the industrial revolution (Albert, 1983). In the nineteenth century railways came to predominate. In both cases, the new transport infrastructure lowered the cost of trade between individuals and firms in different geographical locations. A more specialised spatial division of labour was facilitated, creating new wealth through gains in productivity. By the twentieth century, however, the political climate had changed. In the early 1920s several private consortia proposed a series of new profit-making toll motorways from London to the major cities, usually with the support of local authorities. Maybury, the minister of transport, objected on principle to 'the placing of very important road traffic arteries in the hands of private capitalist enterprise, to be operated for profit' (Plowden, 1971: 193). The construction of the motorway network by the government would have to wait until the 1950s, decades behind Germany, Italy and the United States.

The twentieth century was characterised by a gradual increase in the degree of state involvement in Britain's transport sector. Despite the economic reforms of the 1980s, the trend seems to have continued into the early years of the 21st century. The first section of this chapter therefore examines theoretical objections to the centralised political control of the transport sector. Arguments in favour of government intervention are then discussed: in particular, the contention that since transport imposes economic and environmental costs on society as a whole government needs to act in order to limit these effects. The next section illustrates how government policies have affected the UK transport sector. Finally, different policy options are assessed.

Central planning and political control

In a pure market economy there is division of labour and private ownership of the means of production and there is market exchange of goods and services (Mises, 1949: 238). The operation of the market is not obstructed by institutional factors and the government abstains from hindering its functioning, while protecting it against encroachments on the part of other people. Accordingly there is no interference of factors foreign to the market (ibid.: 239).

It is clear that the transport sector in the UK is very far

removed from such a free market. There is direct political control of rates of fuel duty, road tax and infrastructure expenditure. In addition, numerous centrally decided regulations determine such matters as speed limits, safety provisions, service frequencies, train fares and vehicle sizes. This high degree of central planning and political control inevitably has a profound impact on both the transport sector and the economy as a whole.

According to Austrian economic theory central planning authorities are incapable of making efficient resource allocation decisions. The Misesian critique of socialism suggests that because government decision-makers do not personally own the capital they are allocating they have less incentive to act responsibly or show initiative (Mises, 1935). They lack the 'commercial-mindedness' of private entrepreneurs, in part because the institutional incentive structures within government do not reward this ability. Thus the Victorian railway entrepreneur risked his own property and that of his shareholders when building a new line.[1] In contrast the bureaucrat has little to gain or lose from involvement in a transport project, especially given the extended lines of responsibility typical of government institutions.

The central planners are further hampered because in some of their activities they may not have access to relevant market prices and therefore encounter difficulties in accurately calculating costs and outputs (see Mises, 1949: 696). Transport officials have faced

---

1   The Victorian Railway Bubble of the 1840s might be used as an illustration of market failure and poor planning by entrepreneurs. The investment boom did at least provide Britain with a dense network in a short period of time (see Miller, 2003). It could be argued, however, that the rapid expansion of the railways (and thus the apparent misallocation of resources towards loss-making routes) was facilitated through government intervention in the form of the Parliamentary Acts and the compulsory purchase of land.

this problem when planning new road schemes. In the absence of toll revenue from road users, the true value of the facility to users cannot be known and therefore the rate of return on the capital spent cannot be calculated and vital information about the best way of allocating capital resources is lost. Accordingly, it is unsurprising that transport planners have resorted to deploying extremely complex cost–benefit analyses to help them decide which road schemes are most worthwhile.

The importance of prices is also emphasised in the Hayekian critique of central planning. In his analysis of the use of knowledge in society, Hayek demonstrates how central planners are unable to achieve the most efficient use of resources since they cannot utilise the dispersed and subjective, time- and place-specific knowledge held by every individual (Hayek, 1945). In contrast, markets communicate such information via the price system and thus tend to allocate resources more efficiently and in a pattern that far more accurately reflects the different preferences of individuals.

It can be deduced from the above insights that the misallocation of resources is commonplace within the UK's transport sector, given the high degree of government intervention and central planning. While it is impossible to quantify the impact on the British economy it should be borne in mind that the resulting economic effects could be of far greater magnitude than those simply relating to congestion and pollution. In focusing on the latter issues, writers have arguably neglected transport's integral role in productivity increases and the resulting production of wealth.

The apparent misallocation of transport resources by government will be outlined, by way of illustration, below. Given the negative economic impact of government intervention that can be deduced from Austrian economic theory, however, the next section examines the main justification for state involvement in the industry, namely that transport produces externalities that impose social or environmental costs on the rest of society.

Transport and social cost

Although it can be agreed that in general 'transport prices have been set on the basis of historical precedent or political expediency' (Glaister and Graham, 2005: 633), social cost arguments, taken from welfare economics, are sometimes deployed as a rationale for government intervention in the transport sector. For example, the findings of the Royal Commission on Environmental Pollution report, *Transport and the Environment* (RCEP, 1994), may have played a significant role in the decision to introduce the fuel duty escalator.

Adherents of the social cost approach suggest that, in the light of the external costs associated with transport, Pigouvian taxes might be justified. Additional taxes would be imposed in order to pay for associated economic, environmental and health costs, the rate of taxation being set at a level to maximise the welfare of society as a whole. Thus, transport prices would be partly determined by the state-enforced application of economic science rather than the voluntary decisions of individual participants in freely operating markets. Accordingly, Austrian economists, and many market liberals in general, are quite critical of the social cost approach and its application. Indeed, it is suggested that the deficiencies of social cost arguments may be sufficient to undermine the case for deploying them in policy decisions. An alternative approach, based on enhanced property rights and deregulation, is discussed.

A government determined to set rates of transport taxation and subsidy according to social cost principles would be presented with a number of difficulties. First, it is clear that accurately calculating the social cost of transport is extremely problematic. This is demonstrated by the large degrees of uncertainty observed in studies that attempt to quantify the external costs of road transport in the UK. For example, the influential Royal Commission on Environmental Pollution report estimated the figure at between £10 billion and £18 billion per year. The environmental component of this was between £4.6 billion and £12.9 billion (ibid.: 103). Other studies are characterised by similarly large ranges, if not of environmental costs then of other categories (e.g. Maddison et al., 1996; Sansom et al., 2001). This high level of uncertainty would be problematic were governments to use such calculations to set tax rates, leaving room for significant political discretion in the decision whether to adopt high or low estimates.

Even if a cost estimate could be agreed on, further challenges would arise in the decision regarding which individuals to tax. The level of external costs arising from the transport sector is not simply the result of the actions of individual transport users, when they decide, for example, to take a journey by car. In reality, a complex web of factors is responsible for any given pattern of externalities. For example, the number of people suffering from road noise will depend on the location of the road and its relation to nearby housing. If government planning policies have prevented settlements from adapting to the environmental effects of road transport then they clearly bear part of the responsibility for subsequent negative effects experienced by residents.

A significant proportion of new housing developments continue to be constructed on brown-field sites alongside busy roads and railways despite an abundance of 'set-aside' agricultural land. Yet town planning is just one of numerous factors influencing individuals' experiences of externalities. Any given pattern of external costs from transport is the result of the complex interaction of different government policies and individual actions both current and historical. Thus it is extremely difficult to determine who should pay what to whom in order to remedy the situation. Certainly, it could be argued that a crude tax such as fuel duty is particularly unjust because it bears so little relationship to either the pattern of externalities or the complexity of causative factors.

Given the political pressures facing government decision-makers there is clearly significant potential for arbitrariness in the application of social cost theory to different modes and sectors. While it might be deemed acceptable for road users to pay for accident, congestion and pollution costs the same principle might not be applied to public transport users. Indeed, currently public transport benefits from substantial taxpayer subsidies and the fares are VAT exempt, despite the presence of significant externalities. Notwithstanding environmental costs and accidents, buses, in particular, are responsible for significant spillover effects on other road users – for example, slowing down cars and cyclists.

Moreover, the principle of consistency would demand that social cost principles were applied in the same fashion to all other parts of the economy. From an environmental point of view the energy sector is of particular importance, yet domestic fuel is currently taxed at a very low rate compared with petrol. Although elements of cost–benefit analysis are applied in other sectors (for example, by the National Institute for Health and Clinical

Excellence – NICE – in the health service), it can hardly be argued that the application is consistent, widespread and rigorous.

Thus one policy option would be to extend the scope of taxation based on the environmental/social costs of different activities by consistently applying the principle across all economic sectors. It is debatable, however, to what extent this would be politically practical given that the policy would come into conflict with many egalitarian sensibilities. For example, in the transport sector, the mobility of the less wealthy and the disabled could be affected, while in the energy sector there could be concerns over 'fuel poverty' if domestic energy consumers were paying similar tax rates to motorists.

Egalitarian concerns are also apparent in the estimation of accident costs. There has been a tendency to adopt willingness to pay (WTP) measures of the value of a statistical life (VOSL) in place of gross output measures (for example, by the Department of Transport; Maddison et al., 1996: 127). A perceived problem with the earlier methodology was that the death of a disabled person or retiree could possibly be counted as a benefit since such individuals would tend to have a negative effect on economic output (see ibid.: 125). Yet the very high VOSL values produced by willingness to pay methods (often in the region of £2 million) suggest that they should be treated with scepticism. Certainly, these figures bear no relation to individuals' ability to pay, since only a tiny minority of the population have access to such financial resources. It should also be noted that if the government decided to adopt an unrealistically high VOSL figure, this would tend to exaggerate the social costs of less safe modes such as cars and motorcycles relative to those of trains and buses.

The Contingent Valuation Method (CVM) is the main technique for measuring people's preferences for non-marketed goods and relies on survey data to reveal their willingness to pay for a hypothetical change in their circumstances (ibid.: 34). Yet the CVM is characterised by significant methodological limitations. According to Graves, 'the results will inevitably be affected by the survey design, the scenario presented to the respondents and the possibility that Contingent Valuation responses reflect attitudes rather than real economic commitments' (Graves, 1991: 216). Furthermore, Maddison et al. have noted that 'If respondents realise that the results of this survey will be used to determine the extent of government expenditure they have an incentive to overstate their WTP' (Maddison et al., 1996: 35). Clearly, transport is one sector that people generally assume to be the responsibility of government. While techniques can be deployed to attempt to compensate for such biases, it is doubtful whether the CVM is capable of coming close to simulating the complexity and dynamism of real markets and thereby producing realistic valuations.

These difficulties would appear to make the controversial theoretical position of some Austrian economists relevant to the examination of social cost methodologies. For example, Mises states:

> Prices are a market phenomenon. They are generated by the market process and are the pith of the market economy. There is no such thing as prices outside the market. Prices cannot be constructed synthetically, as it were. They are the resultant of a certain constellation of market data, of actions and reactions of the members of a market society. It is vain to meditate what prices would have been if some of their determinants had been different ... It is no less vain to ponder on what prices ought to be. (Mises, 1949: 392)

Furthermore, there is the problem that social cost studies must translate inherently subjective costs into aggregate monetary terms. Accordingly, Cordato writes,

> [T]he standard approach to environmental economics depends on being able to identify situations where the marginal private benefit of an activity exceeds the marginal social cost. This inherently involves making interpersonal utility comparisons and the summing of interpersonal evaluations across individuals. Neither of these can be held as methodologically valid. (Cordato, 2004: 5)

Clearly, social cost methodologies attempt to measure individual valuations then aggregate them to arrive at a figure for large groups or society as a whole. Yet subjective individual valuations often exhibit significant variation. For example, one person might appreciate a beautiful landscape and another feel nothing. The social cost approach arguably submerges such diverse views and thus, if applied, produces tax rates and prices that fail to reflect the wide variations in individual preferences.[2]

Having criticised the application of social cost methodologies to transport it is worth examining briefly how some of the negative effects associated with the sector might be dealt with in a pure market economy. In the absence of government intervention many environmental effects could be priced via land and property markets. Accordingly, different environmental options could be made available for individuals with different preferences.[3] For

---

[2] It might also be added that individuals often value their surroundings and circumstances in terms of an order of preference and do not value them in monetary terms. Thus social cost studies could be accused of falsely imputing to individuals monetary figures that would not exist outside the research environment.

[3] For a detailed discussion of the possibilities of private land-use planning, see Pennington (2002).

example, a developer of new housing settlements would have a strong incentive to provide a suitable transport infrastructure to provide access to the properties. If a new railway line were constructed as part of the scheme then residential properties alongside the route could be sold at a cheaper price than those farther away, in order to reflect the additional noise and air pollution adjacent residents might expect to endure. Thus the external costs of the railway effectively would be given a market price arrived at through voluntary agreement.

There would also be strong incentives for any developer to invest in the environmental qualities of the new settlement according to the tastes of potential property buyers. Binding restrictions could be imposed by the developer to reduce the negative impacts of transport. For example, trains and lorries could be banned from entering the settlement for a period at night. Motorcycles could be prohibited completely. Older, noisier and more polluting cars could be excluded. The precise mix of measures would depend on the developer's best estimate of the preferences of property buyers for different environmental goods. Clearly such market-based solutions are dependent on deregulated land development, the private ownership of new transport links and the concomitant return of the close relationship between new transport infrastructure and property development.[4]

In the absence of state intervention, markets are capable of pricing many external effects of transport and thereby providing incentives to reduce their magnitude. This is particularly clear in the case of congestion, which is estimated to cost the UK economy

---

[4] The principles of private property and voluntary exchange could also make a significant contribution to reducing the possible eventual impact of large-scale environmental problems such as climate change.

in excess of £21 billion per year, more than all the other road traffic externalities put together (Blythe, 2005: 572).[5] Freely operating markets are capable of eliminating congestion through increased user charges at busy times, enhanced infrastructure capacity, the geographical dispersal of economic activity, or some combination of the above and other measures. Accordingly, it is possible to contend that, like environmental costs, current congestion levels are primarily the result of government policies that prevent the efficient operation of transport and land markets. Thus, even if one accepts their methodological validity, it can be argued that since social cost studies are situated in the context of the current highly regulated policy framework they actually provide very little information about the external costs of transport in an unhampered market economy.

Transport and poverty

The alleviation of relative poverty provides another important rationale for government involvement in the transport sector. For egalitarians, transport policy is about giving 'access' to all sections of the 'community', including women, pensioners on low incomes, those with young children, the disabled and members of ethnic minorities (Prescott, 1992; Torrance, 1992). A market-based system is therefore rejected for its inherent inequalities.

Yet it is far from clear that government intervention benefits low-income groups. Regulation and taxation may have inflated the costs of car ownership beyond the reach of many, through

---

5 It should be noted that congestion costs are generally excluded from fully allocated cost analyses since they are not external to road users as a group (see Sansom et al., 2001).

fuel duty, road tax, compulsory insurance, increasingly complex driving tests, vehicle design standards, import restrictions and MOT tests. At the same time, state regulation has prevented the development of the low-cost forms of transport seen in the Third World, such as shared taxis and driver-owned minibuses. These options could significantly reduce any disadvantages faced by those unable to drive. Furthermore, it should be noted that expenditure on public transport has tended to be concentrated on the railways, subsidising, *inter alia*, commuters, business travellers and those who live in the countryside:[6] none of these groups is necessarily poor.

There are, however, elements of British policy that are more clearly directed at addressing inequalities in transport. These include bus subsidies, free passes for the elderly, reduced fares for children, students and families, and mobility allowances for the disabled. But it is not clear that such measures are sufficient to ameliorate the negative effects of taxation and regulation mentioned above. Furthermore, as subsidies from taxpayers, these policies are economically damaging because resources are transferred from the productive parts of the economy to the non-productive, thereby reducing the growth of the former. Moreover, incentive structures are altered such that it becomes more attractive for individuals to remain dependent on the state for their travel and other wants. Finally, if it is desired to transfer resources to such groups, it is much more efficient to transfer cash than to provide benefits in kind such as subsidised transport by certain modes.

---

6   Rural railways are particularly heavily subsidised.

The privatised railway

The economic problems associated with central planning and political control have been illustrated on Britain's railways during the past decade. Although British Rail was ostensibly privatised in the mid-1990s, the heavy degree of regulation and subsidy applied to the industry meant that the prevailing economic conditions were very far removed from those that would be expected in an unhampered market. Indeed, the privatisation of British Rail was perhaps analogous to what Hayek termed 'constructivist rationalism' in the social sphere (Hayek, 1988). A complex web of contracts, institutions and regulations was artificially created that would never have evolved spontaneously through voluntary exchange under market conditions. Furthermore, the design of this structure cost the taxpayer £450 million in consultancy fees (Wolmar, 2001: 75). Unfortunately the perceived failures of the privatised railway have, rather unfairly, brought the whole process of privatisation, and even free markets themselves, into disrepute. Thus it becomes essential to examine the role of government intervention in the rail sector, and in particular in those areas where the results of privatisation have come under most criticism.

Before starting this analysis it is necessary to describe the main elements of the privatised railway. The traditional vertically integrated structure of the industry, in which the owner of the tracks also ran the trains, was discarded in favour of a system that deliberately segregated the different roles. Ownership of the tracks was given to Railtrack, a company that was floated on the stock market in 1996. The government sold the trains, the locomotives, carriages and wagons, to specially created rolling-stock companies (ROSCOs). The vehicles were then leased to the train operating companies (TOCs), which were given the responsibility for actually running the train services. The TOCs were awarded franchises for given routes by the government, initially through the Office of Passenger Railway Franchising (OPRAF). A Rail Regulator was appointed to oversee the industry.

Following the election of a Labour government in 1997 there were some structural changes to the industry. In 1999 the Strategic Rail Authority was created to coordinate future expenditure on the network and replace OPRAF as the agency responsible for the franchising process. In 2001 the government forced Railtrack into liquidation. It was replaced by Network Rail, a not-for-profit company, in a de facto renationalisation of the track and stations. The Strategic Rail Authority was earmarked for abolition in the 2004 Rail Review, with its functions transferred to the Department for Transport (DfT).

The level of government subsidy for the industry has risen considerably since the mid-1990s despite initial hopes that efficiency savings would in the medium term reduce the demand for taxpayer support (ibid.). The responsibility for this outcome clearly lies, however, with state interference. The 1993 Railways Act made it virtually impossible to close loss-making lines even though these routes could potentially have been valuable if Railtrack had sold them as development property or converted them into toll roads (offering unimpeded access to town centres in many cases). According to one estimate, 'marginal lines' account for just 17 per cent of rail travel but 64 per cent of operating subsidy.[7]

While this statistic suggests that line closures would substantially reduce the need for taxpayer funding, it is important to remember that in the absence of unhampered competition among

---

7   Reported in 'Rail network set for further cuts', *Observer*, 2 March 2003.

different transport modes it is impossible to properly assess the market value of currently loss-making railways. Furthermore, in the absence of state regulation of safety it is likely that currently loss-making lines could reduce their costs significantly.

Indeed, high expenditure on rail safety is one reason why the rate of subsidy has risen. In 1999 the government decided to roll out a new Train Protection and Warning System across the network at the cost of £585 million, or an estimated £15.4 million per life saved (CfIT, 2004). The Hatfield crash of 2000, which killed four people, less than half the daily average fatalities on Britain's roads, led to even more expenditure on safety, including an emergency track renewal programme and speed restrictions (which led to large compensation payments from Railtrack to the train-operating companies), and eventually promoted the adoption of the £3.7 billion European Rail Traffic Management System, estimated to cost £99.2 million per passenger life saved (ibid.).[8]

In terms of government expenditure it would appear that such additional spending on passenger safety is particularly wasteful. Serious accidents on the railway are rare, and the same money would save far more lives if spent elsewhere. Better still, if the rail safety subsidies were converted into tax cuts then taxpayers could decide for themselves whether to spend their additional resources on improving their health and safety or alternatively on something else more important to them. Of course, in an unhampered market a private railway owner might wish to spend large

---

8 The CfIT reduces this figure to £13.2 million per life saved by including benefits from the new system of increased capacity and punctuality. If greater capacity leads to more trains running, however, this is likely to increase the level of taxpayer subsidy, creating an additional cost.

amounts on safety in order to prevent his company's reputation being damaged by a major accident. In the absence of taxpayer subsidy, however, safety expenditure would have to be carefully balanced against its impact on passenger fares in the context of free competition from other transport modes.

Still greater costs have resulted from the government's desire for the railway to transport a greater share of passenger and freight traffic. The government's 10 Year Transport Plan aimed to increase passenger traffic by 80 per cent and freight by 50 per cent by 2010 (DETR, 2000). Meeting this ambition (now abandoned) entailed improving the quality and increasing the capacity of certain parts of the rail network, at enormous cost to the taxpayer. The cost of upgrading the West Coast Main Line (WCML), which links London, Birmingham, Manchester and Glasgow, will be £7.6 billion, according to recent estimates (Hudson, 2004). Extrapolating from the cost of section one of the Channel Tunnel Rail Link (CTRL), it seems likely that a brand-new high-speed railway could have been built at similar cost, at least as far as Lancashire.[9] Alternatively, the sum could have paid for the construction of approximately 500 miles of six-lane motorway. Once again, the WCML modernisation project appears to provide evidence of the wasteful allocation of resources. Although the scheme was started under Railtrack, it should be noted that the company was required by the Rail Regulator to spend a certain share of its turnover on infrastructure renewal.

Regulation also played a key role in reducing the income of the rail industry, and thereby increasing the need for subsidy,

---

9   Section one of the CTRL cost £1.9 billion for 46 miles of double track for 186 mph running (see www.ctrl.co.uk), compared with 125 mph on the modernised WCML.

through the capping of fares. Season tickets, off-peak savers and fares for all journeys within 50 miles of London were regulated. Thus as demand rose in the late 1990s, these fares could not rise to choke it off, with chronic congestion, especially on peak-time London commuter trains, the predictable result. This congestion led to demands for increased capacity on the worst-affected routes. The state-imposed structure created further problems, however. According to Wolmar: '[The system] is very unwieldy ... with only 9 per cent of the charges being variable. In other words, Railtrack gets very little extra money (and in many cases none at all) when additional trains are run on its tracks, a situation which was to cause the company much grief when operators started putting on many new services in the late 1990s' (Wolmar, 2001: 96).

Thus there was little economic incentive for Railtrack to earmark expenditure for increasing capacity. Furthermore, the increased traffic actually cost Railtrack money through increased wear and tear on the system. The transmission of passenger wants via the price mechanism was precluded by fare regulation and the artificial structure of the industry. In a pure market economy there would be many options open to railway owners faced with a substantial increase in passenger demand. They could increase fares, increase capacity or apply a combination of the two, depending on which they thought would give them the highest return. The amount of congestion experienced by passengers would in part depend on their willingness to pay to avoid it (for example, if the market supported it, railway owners could introduce high-density standing-only carriages for those willing to sacrifice comfort for a cheaper journey).

If the price mechanism had been allowed to operate freely then Railtrack would have been able to raise track charges in response to the greater passenger demands on its infrastructure. Yet this ability to raise prices in an unregulated market provides a powerful argument against the degree of separation of ownership and function seen on Britain's privatised railway. In an unhampered market the owner of the tracks would have the whip hand over the train-operating companies. If the latter succeeded in increasing their profits by attracting more passengers then there would be nothing to stop the track owner from raising its prices in order to increase its profits. Given this possibility, the owners of train-operating companies would want the track owner's charges and obligations set out in a contract before investing their capital. Given the potential costs associated with such a contract, however, such as transaction costs and a loss in operational flexibility, it is difficult to see why the track owner would wish to enter into such an agreement, except where substantial efficiency gains would be achieved by the separation of track and train (for example, when long-distance services made use of many different owners' tracks). Railway owners would have to trade off the profit from allowing other companies to use their tracks with the resulting additional costs. They might also consider whether they could profit more by providing the proposed train services themselves. The main point is that, in contrast to Britain's railway, in an unhampered market guided by prices, the degree of vertical integration could be adjusted according to the changing demands on the network.

Distorted competition

Given the very high degree of government intervention in the railway industry it is very difficult to determine whether different parts of the rail network are economically viable. The problem is compounded by government measures that impede free competition with other modes of transport. The high level of taxpayer subsidy has already been mentioned. On long-distance routes, such as London to Paris and London to Glasgow, the trains are competing directly with the airlines, yet the railways are receiving capital grants from government to improve infrastructure: this situation hardly constitutes fair competition. At the same time, when the private sector attempts to increase capacity at airports, it is faced with very great obstacles in the planning system, as demonstrated by the long-running and highly expensive public inquiry into Terminal Five at Heathrow.

On many other intercity routes trains compete directly with coaches. Unlike many train services, however, the latter do not receive an operating subsidy or the fuel duty rebate accorded to buses (Hibbs, 2000). Coaches are further disadvantaged by an EU-imposed speed limit that restricts them to 62 mph, even on motorways, despite their inherent safety (ibid.). Moreover, since motorways and trunk roads are free at the point of use and because the supply of road infrastructure has been determined by government diktat rather than the marginal demand for road space, coaches are slowed down by congestion. If coaches travelled at 80 mph on uncongested routes and perhaps used the edge-of-city terminals found in many developing countries, then they could provide very serious competition for the railways. Lower top speeds might be compensated by lower fares, increased service frequencies and a greater variety of routes, including direct journeys to smaller towns badly served by rail.

Despite the advantages of deregulated intercity coaches compared with trains, there can be no guarantee that either mode would be economically viable in an unhampered market system.

Coaches, like trains, benefit from the VAT exemption on public transport fares. The main source of uncertainty as to the underlying competitive position of public transport, however, is the high level of government involvement in the activities of private road users. Motorists, in particular, are very heavily taxed. In 2003 tax revenues from fuel duty and road tax exceeded government expenditure on the road network by £20 billion,[10] a sum large enough to construct about 1,500 miles of six-lane motorway (DfT, 2004). It is inconceivable that such a rate of construction, carried out, for example, over the last twenty years, would not have reduced congestion significantly, especially if a more liberal planning system had allowed economic activity to take full advantage of the available capacity through dispersal from cramped inner cities with their narrow Victorian streets. It is also difficult to deny that a far more specialised and productive geographical division of labour would have been achieved in Britain if the government had reserved its road user tax receipts for road expenditure.

The magnitude of fuel duty revenue suggests that motorists are prepared to pay significant sums for the use of road space. In the absence of market prices on the road network, however, it is impossible to know the actual amount of road space that would have been provided in an unhampered market economy or what charges motorists would voluntarily pay for using it. Whether railways or other public transport modes could survive deregulation and the removal of differential taxes, subsidies and regulations cannot be determined with absolute certainty in advance.

---

10 If the VAT on fuel duty is included the sum is nearly £24 billion.

Towards free competition in transport

A key lesson that can be drawn from the recent history of Britain's railways is that if government intervenes in market processes then many of the benefits expected from privatisation will be to some degree undermined. The current situation, in which general taxpayers, many of whom never use trains, subsidise rail passengers, is difficult to justify, even in egalitarian or environmental terms (see above). In addition, much of the expenditure on rail may be considered economically wasteful since a commercial return on the investment will never be achieved. Moreover, the central direction of rail expenditure by government officials means that, to a significant extent, it is detached from the wants of transport consumers and subject to the influence of special interest lobbies.

In order to end the requirement for subsidising the railways, it will be necessary to allow unprofitable lines and services to be closed. Furthermore, it should be possible for the market to determine the appropriate level of vertical integration on the network. Thus, if operating companies wish to take over the tracks and stations they use, the government should permit this provided subsidies are ended.[11]

In order to encourage fair competition between modes, government should also seek to moderate the burden of safety regulations on the railways, enabling the industry to reduce costs significantly. The railway owners would be able to decide how much to spend on safety themselves according to their perception of its importance as indicated by consumer demand.

Wider reforms could also help the rail sector's competitive-

---

11 Allowing train operators to take over the tracks when their passenger services are heavily subsidised could unfairly disadvantage rail freight operations.

ness. A liberalisation of employment law would help reduce the wage inflation that has hampered parts of the industry since privatisation. Similarly, an end to the special legal exemptions applying to trade unions would be beneficial (the rail industry remains heavily unionised compared with many competing transport modes).

Some railways could also benefit from the liberalisation of planning controls in central London to allow the development of skyscrapers and high-rise residential blocks, since it seems unlikely that such schemes could be served adequately by private motor vehicles. At the same time, increased private residential development in Inner London could actually harm the profitability of the commuter lines. A liberalised planning system is also an essential element in restoring the traditional link between transport infrastructure and property development. Without green belts and other restrictions, railway owners could fund infrastructure improvements and the maintenance of services by developing land along new routes and stations. This process would be particularly attractive around London since mass commuting by road into central London is clearly impractical given current infrastructure provision and urban form. Under these conditions there seems every reason to believe that the London commuter railways would thrive in the absence of subsidies and government regulation.[12]

Similarly, many of the intercity rail routes from central London might be viable since the distances involved are probably too short for air to compete on overall journey times. Higher-speed coach

---

[12] A major caveat is that rail companies might be able to increase capacity and reduce costs by converting commuter tracks into dedicated bus routes (see Withrington, 2004). The routes could also be used by toll-paying private cars and goods vehicles, possibly at off-peak times, thereby boosting revenues.

services on uncongested roads could, however, present problems for the intercity operators. The airlines might also drive the train companies out of business on the London–Scotland routes, although, in the absence of government intervention, the outcome would depend on passenger preferences.

Liberalisation and private ownership could also lead to greater integration between different modes. The cross-ownership of trains and buses is already very much in evidence with companies like Stagecoach and National Express. It would be in a rail firm's interests to provide feeder bus services to their trunk routes in situations where branch lines had been closed to passenger traffic. Furthermore, depending on consumer demand, it might be beneficial for the railways to integrate their services more fully with the demands of the motor car, for example by moving major stations out of town, perhaps to locations where railway lines and motorways intersected. Many potential rail users, particularly business travellers, no longer live in inner-city areas. It is a deterrent to rail use that they must travel through congested urban streets to reach a major station and then pay expensive parking charges if they have decided to drive there. New out-of-town 'parkway' stations might enable many branch lines to be closed while actually improving overall travel times for many passengers. There would of course be extensive opportunities for property development at the new sites. New town centres would effectively be created that were purpose built to make efficient use of modern transport technology. Any disused railways could be converted into dedicated bus routes or toll roads, or the land could be developed, depending on which option offered the greatest commercial return. One of the great advantages of a proper market in transport infrastructure is that existing routes could be used far more efficiently, in many cases avoiding the high costs of developing brand-new links.

In order to maximise the comparability of prices between different transport modes it is essential that any liberalisation of the railways is accompanied by a similar policy on the road network. Unfortunately, the privatisation of residential roads presents many difficulties in terms of both charging methods and access rights to private property, and is therefore likely to be a piecemeal process that would take many decades.[13] In contrast, the privatisation of the motorways and parts of the trunk road network appears to be relatively straightforward and achievable. The political control of the road privatisation process brings with it, however, a number of dangers.

A national road-charging system based on satellite tracking technology has been advocated as a possible stepping stone towards increasing the role of the private sector in the provision of road infrastructure. While this system would probably reduce congestion problems it would not respond to consumer demands for more road infrastructure. Indeed, it has been suggested that a possible benefit of a national charging system would be the reduced need for new road capacity (Glaister and Graham, 2004: 109). One can imagine the economic damage that would have occurred if such a system had been put in place in 1930. Instead of building trunk roads, and eventually motorways, prices would have been raised on the existing infrastructure to avoid congestion.

---

13 The privatisation of residential roads could start by allowing the developers or inhabitants of new private housing estates to retain ownership of the roads and thereby control access to the properties in order to exclude criminals. Clearly it would be unjust if householders in such estates had to pay council tax for services provided privately. Thus the privatisation of residential roads would also require significant structural reforms to local authorities.

The production of wealth through a greater geographical division of labour would have been seriously impeded by artificially high transport costs. There can be no guarantee that a national charging system would not have a similar negative economic effect in the future.[14]

Notwithstanding the very grave implications for civil liberties, the political control of a national charging system would undoubtedly lead to calls for special exemptions for 'key workers' and 'deprived areas', or alternatively compensatory regeneration funding or potentially very large public transport subsidies. While the exact redistributive effects of a charging system are difficult to predict it seems likely that much of the economic benefit gained from reducing congestion would be absorbed by such payments.

A pure privatisation of motorways and trunk roads could avoid many of the problems discussed above since the level of tolls would be the concern of the road owners and therefore outside political control. Of course, it would be preferable if fuel duty were dramatically reduced, or the tax abolished, since otherwise drivers would be paying over the market rate for using the private roads. The continuation of high fuel taxes would seriously undermine the economics of new road construction since revenue that could be gained by the road owner through tolls would be diverted to the government.

Furthermore, it is preferable that the proceeds of privatisation

---

14 Though it should be mentioned that charges do provide the information to potential investors about consumer preferences for road space and therefore the profitability of new roads. This argument is not an argument against pricing as such but an argument against pricing in the absence of the liberalisation of constraints on new road building (see below). It is also an argument against the use of a government-controlled pricing scheme that would provide incentives for government to restrict road building to maximise its monopoly profits.

are not absorbed by the Treasury but instead are distributed to road users (for example, holders of driving licences or registered vehicle owners could receive shares in the new road companies). If this were not done, the government would have a strong incentive to restrict the construction of new roads by competitors in order to inflate artificially the value of the existing road infrastructure and maximise its receipts from any flotation. Likewise, it is essential that potential private road builders are able to operate in a liberal planning environment such that the government cannot use the planning system to direct transport policy by the back door (for example, by banning or delaying road construction but allowing public transport schemes). In the absence of these regulatory and fiscal conditions it is likely that the benefits of road privatisation will be severely limited and may serve to bring free markets further undeserved criticism.

Conclusion

Britain's railways were born in an era of entrepreneurship and individualism. Like other industries, however, they gradually became subject to a greater degree of government intervention culminating in the nationalisation of 1947. Unfortunately, privatisation did not fully reverse this process. Instead the railways were so tightly regulated that many of the benefits deriving from markets were lost. Free markets were unfairly brought into disrepute and in consequence future withdrawals of state involvement in economic activities have been made more politically difficult.

In fact, the problems of the privatised railway have clearly illustrated the perils of centralised political control. The misallocation of resources has become endemic, as demonstrated by the high level of taxpayer subsidy. Only the liberalisation of the entire transport sector will reveal which parts of the railway will have a long-term future as genuinely profitable businesses. While such a policy would take a good deal of political courage, the proposed reductions in fuel duty and the wide distribution of road shares could help sway public opinion in its favour.

References

Albert, W. (1983), 'The turnpike trusts', in D. H. Aldcroft and M. J. Freeman (eds), *Transport in the Industrial Revolution*, Manchester: Manchester University Press.

Blythe, P. T. (2005), 'Congestion charging: technical options for the delivery of future UK policy', *Transportation Research Part A*, 39: 571–87.

CfIT (Commission for Integrated Transport) (2004), 'Rail safety: revision of factsheet 10', available at www.cfit.gov.uk/research/railsafety/03.htm.

Cordato, R. E. (2004), 'Towards an Austrian theory of environmental economics', *Quarterly Journal of Austrian Economics*, 7(1): 3–16.

DETR (Department of the Environment, Transport and the Regions) (2000), *Transport 2010: The 10 Year Plan*, London: HMSO.

DfT (Department for Transport) (2004), *Transport Statistics Great Britain*, London: HMSO.

Glaister, S. and D. J. Graham (2004), *Pricing Our Roads: Vision and Reality*, London: Institute of Economic Affairs.

Glaister, S. and D. J. Graham (2005), 'An evaluation of national road user charging in England', *Transportation Research Part A*, 39: 632–50.

Graves, P. E. (1991), 'Aesthetics', in J. B. Braden and C. D. Kolstad (eds), *Measuring the Demand for Environmental Quality*, Amsterdam/New York: North Holland.

Hayek, F. A. (1945), 'The use of knowledge in society', *American Economic Review*, XXXV(4): 519–30.

Hayek, F. A. (1988), *The Fatal Conceit: The Errors of Socialism*, London: Routledge.

Hibbs, J. (2000), *Transport Policy: The Myth of Integrated Planning*, London: Institute of Economic Affairs.

Hudson, G. (2004), 'The West Coast: in the home straight?', *Modern Railways*, June, pp. 52–4.

Maddison, D., D. Pearce, O. Johansson, E. Calthrop, T. Litman and E. Verhoef (1996), *Blueprint 5: The True Costs of Road Transport*, London: Earthscan.

Miller, R. C. B. (2003), *railway.com. Parallels between the early British railways and the ICT revolution*, London: Institute of Economic Affairs.

Mises, L. (1935), 'Economic calculation in the socialist commonwealth', in F. A. Hayek (ed.), *Collectivist Economic Planning: Critical Studies of the Possibilities of Socialism*, London: Routledge & Kegan Paul, pp. 87–130.

Mises, L. (1949), *Human Action: A Treatise on Economics*, London: William Hodge.

Pennington, M. (2002), *Liberating the Land: The Case for Private Land-use Planning*, London: Institute of Economic Affairs.

Plowden, W. (1971), *The Motor Car and Politics, 1896–1970*, London: Bodley Head.

Prescott, J. (1992), 'Foreword', in J. Roberts, J. Cleary, K. Hamilton and J. Hanna (eds), *Travel Sickness: The need for a sustainable transport policy for Britain*, London: Lawrence and Wishart.

RCEP (Royal Commission on Environmental Pollution) (1994), *Transport and the Environment*, 18th report, London: HMSO.

Sansom, T., C. Nash, P. Mackie, J. Shires and P. Watkiss (2001), *Surface Transport Costs and Charges: Great Britain 1998*, Leeds: Institute for Transport Studies.

Torrance, H. (1992), 'Transport for all. Equal opportunities in transport policy', in J. Roberts, J. Cleary, K. Hamilton and J. Hanna (eds), *Travel Sickness: The need for a sustainable transport policy for Britain*, London: Lawrence and Wishart.

Withrington, P. F. (2004), 'Reigniting the railway conversion debate', *Economic Affairs*, 24(2).

Wolmar, C. (2001), *Broken Rails: How Privatisation Wrecked Britain's Railways*, London: Aurum Press.

ABOUT THE IEA

The Institute is a research and educational charity (No. CC 235 351), limited by guarantee. Its mission is to improve understanding of the fundamental institutions of a free society with particular reference to the role of markets in solving economic and social problems.

The IEA achieves its mission by:

- a high-quality publishing programme
- conferences, seminars, lectures and other events
- outreach to school and college students
- brokering media introductions and appearances

The IEA, which was established in 1955 by the late Sir Antony Fisher, is an educational charity, not a political organisation. It is independent of any political party or group and does not carry on activities intended to affect support for any political party or candidate in any election or referendum, or at any other time. It is financed by sales of publications, conference fees and voluntary donations.

In addition to its main series of publications the IEA also publishes a quarterly journal, *Economic Affairs*.

The IEA is aided in its work by a distinguished international Academic Advisory Council and an eminent panel of Honorary Fellows. Together with other academics, they review prospective IEA publications, their comments being passed on anonymously to authors. All IEA papers are therefore subject to the same rigorous independent refereeing process as used by leading academic journals.

IEA publications enjoy widespread classroom use and course adoptions in schools and universities. They are also sold throughout the world and often translated/reprinted.

Since 1974 the IEA has helped to create a world-wide network of 100 similar institutions in over 70 countries. They are all independent but share the IEA's mission.

Views expressed in the IEA's publications are those of the authors, not those of the Institute (which has no corporate view), its Managing Trustees, Academic Advisory Council members or senior staff.

Members of the Institute's Academic Advisory Council, Honorary Fellows, Trustees and Staff are listed on the following page.

The Institute gratefully acknowledges financial support for its publications programme and other work from a generous benefaction by the late Alec and Beryl Warren.

The Institute of Economic Affairs
2 Lord North Street, Westminster, London SW1P 3LB
Tel: 020 7799 8900
Fax: 020 7799 2137
Email: iea@iea.org.uk
Internet: iea.org.uk

Director General	John Blundell
Editorial Director	Professor Philip Booth

Managing Trustees

Chairman: Professor D R Myddelton

Kevin Bell
Robert Boyd
Michael Fisher
Michael Hintze
Malcolm McAlpine

Professor Patrick Minford
Professor Martin Ricketts
Professor J R Shackleton
Sir Peter Walters
Linda Whetstone

Academic Advisory Council

Chairman: Professor Martin Ricketts

Graham Bannock
Professor Norman Barry
Dr Roger Bate
Professor Donald J Boudreaux
Professor John Burton
Professor Forrest Capie
Professor Steven N S Cheung
Professor Tim Congdon
Professor N F R Crafts
Professor David de Meza
Professor Kevin Dowd
Professor Richard A Epstein
Nigel Essex
Professor David Greenaway
Dr Ingrid A Gregg
Walter E Grinder
Professor Steve H Hanke
Professor Keith Hartley
Professor David Henderson
Professor Peter M Jackson
Dr Jerry Jordan
Dr Lynne Kiesling
Professor Daniel B Klein

Dr Anja Kluever
Professor Stephen C Littlechild
Dr Eileen Marshall
Professor Antonio Martino
Julian Morris
Paul Ormerod
Professor David Parker
Dr Mark Pennington
Professor Victoria Curzon Price
Professor Colin Robinson
Professor Charles K Rowley
Professor Pascal Salin
Dr Razeen Sally
Professor Pedro Schwartz
Jane S Shaw
Professor W Stanley Siebert
Dr Elaine Sternberg
Professor James Tooley
Professor Nicola Tynan
Professor Roland Vaubel
Professor Lawrence H White
Professor Walter E Williams
Professor Geoffrey E Wood

Honorary Fellows

Professor Armen A Alchian
Professor Michael Beenstock
Sir Samuel Brittan
Professor James M Buchanan
Professor Ronald H Coase
Dr R M Hartwell
Professor Terence W Hutchison
Professor David Laidler
Professor Dennis S Lees

Professor Chiaki Nishiyama
Professor Sir Alan Peacock
Professor Ben Roberts
Professor Anna J Schwartz
Professor Vernon L Smith
Professor Gordon Tullock
Professor Sir Alan Walters
Professor Basil S Yamey

Other papers recently published by the IEA include:

WHO, What and Why?
Transnational Government, Legitimacy and the World Health Organization
Roger Scruton
Occasional Paper 113; ISBN 0 255 36487 3
£8.00

The World Turned Rightside Up
A New Trading Agenda for the Age of Globalisation
John C. Hulsman
Occasional Paper 114; ISBN 0 255 36495 4
£8.00

The Representation of Business in English Literature
Introduced and edited by Arthur Pollard
Readings 53; ISBN 0 255 36491 1
£12.00

Anti-Liberalism 2000
The Rise of New Millennium Collectivism
David Henderson
Occasional Paper 115; ISBN 0 255 36497 0
£7.50

Capitalism, Morality and Markets
Brian Griffiths, Robert A. Sirico, Norman Barry & Frank Field
Readings 54; ISBN 0 255 36496 2
£7.50

A Conversation with Harris and Seldon
Ralph Harris & Arthur Seldon
Occasional Paper 116; ISBN 0 255 36498 9
£7.50

Malaria and the DDT Story
Richard Tren & Roger Bate
Occasional Paper 117; ISBN 0 255 36499 7
£10.00

A Plea to Economists Who Favour Liberty: Assist the Everyman
Daniel B. Klein
Occasional Paper 118; ISBN 0 255 36501 2
£10.00

The Changing Fortunes of Economic Liberalism
Yesterday, Today and Tomorrow
David Henderson
Occasional Paper 105 (new edition); ISBN 0 255 36520 9
£12.50

The Global Education Industry
Lessons from Private Education in Developing Countries
James Tooley
Hobart Paper 141 (new edition); ISBN 0 255 36503 9
£12.50

Saving Our Streams
The Role of the Anglers' Conservation Association in
Protecting English and Welsh Rivers
Roger Bate
Research Monograph 53; ISBN 0 255 36494 6
£10.00

Better Off Out?
The Benefits or Costs of EU Membership
Brian Hindley & Martin Howe
Occasional Paper 99 (new edition); ISBN 0 255 36502 0
£10.00

Buckingham at 25
Freeing the Universities from State Control
Edited by James Tooley
Readings 55; ISBN 0 255 36512 8
£15.00

Lectures on Regulatory and Competition Policy
Irwin M. Stelzer
Occasional Paper 120; ISBN 0 255 36511 X
£12.50

Misguided Virtue
False Notions of Corporate Social Responsibility
David Henderson
Hobart Paper 142; ISBN 0 255 36510 1
£12.50

HIV and Aids in Schools
The Political Economy of Pressure Groups and Miseducation
Barrie Craven, Pauline Dixon, Gordon Stewart & James Tooley
Occasional Paper 121; ISBN 0 255 36522 5
£10.00

The Road to Serfdom
The Reader's Digest *condensed version*
Friedrich A. Hayek
Occasional Paper 122; ISBN 0 255 36530 6
£7.50

Bastiat's *The Law*
Introduction by Norman Barry
Occasional Paper 123; ISBN 0 255 36509 8
£7.50

A Globalist Manifesto for Public Policy
Charles Calomiris
Occasional Paper 124; ISBN 0 255 36525 X
£7.50

Euthanasia for Death Duties
Putting Inheritance Tax Out of Its Misery
Barry Bracewell-Milnes
Research Monograph 54; ISBN 0 255 36513 6
£10.00

Liberating the Land
The Case for Private Land-use Planning
Mark Pennington
Hobart Paper 143; ISBN 0 255 36508 x
£10.00

IEA Yearbook of Government Performance 2002/2003
Edited by Peter Warburton
Yearbook 1; ISBN 0 255 36532 2
£15.00

Britain's Relative Economic Performance, 1870–1999
Nicholas Crafts
Research Monograph 55; ISBN 0 255 36524 1
£10.00

Should We Have Faith in Central Banks?
Otmar Issing
Occasional Paper 125; ISBN 0 255 36528 4
£7.50

The Dilemma of Democracy
Arthur Seldon
Hobart Paper 136 (reissue); ISBN 0 255 36536 5
£10.00

Capital Controls: a 'Cure' Worse Than the Problem?
Forrest Capie
Research Monograph 56; ISBN 0 255 36506 3
£10.00

The Poverty of 'Development Economics'
Deepak Lal
Hobart Paper 144 (reissue); ISBN 0 255 36519 5
£15.00

Should Britain Join the Euro?
The Chancellor's Five Tests Examined
Patrick Minford
Occasional Paper 126; ISBN 0 255 36527 6
£7.50

Post-Communist Transition: Some Lessons
Leszek Balcerowicz
Occasional Paper 127; ISBN 0 255 36533 0
£7.50

A Tribute to Peter Bauer
John Blundell et al.
Occasional Paper 128; ISBN 0 255 36531 4
£10.00

Employment Tribunals
Their Growth and the Case for Radical Reform
J. R. Shackleton
Hobart Paper 145; ISBN 0 255 36515 2
£10.00

Fifty Economic Fallacies Exposed

Geoffrey E. Wood
Occasional Paper 129; ISBN 0 255 36518 7
£12.50

A Market in Airport Slots

Keith Boyfield (editor), David Starkie, Tom Bass & Barry Humphreys
Readings 56; ISBN 0 255 36505 5
£10.00

Money, Inflation and the Constitutional Position of the Central Bank

Milton Friedman & Charles A. E. Goodhart
Readings 57; ISBN 0 255 36538 1
£10.00

railway.com

Parallels between the Early British Railways and the ICT Revolution
Robert C. B. Miller
Research Monograph 57; ISBN 0 255 36534 9
£12.50

The Regulation of Financial Markets

Edited by Philip Booth & David Currie
Readings 58; ISBN 0 255 36551 9
£12.50

Climate Alarmism Reconsidered
Robert L. Bradley Jr
Hobart Paper 146; ISBN 0 255 36541 1
£12.50

Government Failure: E. G. West on Education
Edited by James Tooley & James Stanfield
Occasional Paper 130; ISBN 0 255 36552 7
£12.50

Waging the War of Ideas
John Blundell
Second edition
Occasional Paper 131; ISBN 0 255 36547 0
£12.50

Corporate Governance: Accountability in the Marketplace
Elaine Sternberg
Second edition
Hobart Paper 147; ISBN 0 255 36542 X
£12.50

The Land Use Planning System
Evaluating Options for Reform
John Corkindale
Hobart Paper 148; ISBN 0 255 36550 0
£10.00

Economy and Virtue
Essays on the Theme of Markets and Morality
Edited by Dennis O'Keeffe
Readings 59; ISBN 0 255 36504 7
£12.50

Free Markets Under Siege
Cartels, Politics and Social Welfare
Richard A. Epstein
Occasional Paper 132; ISBN 0 255 36553 5
£10.00

Unshackling Accountants
D. R. Myddelton
Hobart Paper 149; ISBN 0 255 36559 4
£12.50

The Euro as Politics
Pedro Schwartz
Research Monograph 58; ISBN 0 255 36535 7
£12.50

Pricing Our Roads
Vision and Reality
Stephen Glaister & Daniel J. Graham
Research Monograph 59; ISBN 0 255 36562 4
£10.00

The Role of Business in the Modern World
Progress, Pressures, and Prospects for the Market Economy
David Henderson
Hobart Paper 150; ISBN 0 255 36548 9
£12.50

Public Service Broadcasting Without the BBC?
Alan Peacock
Occasional Paper 133; ISBN 0 255 36565 9
£10.00

The ECB and the Euro: the First Five Years
Otmar Issing
Occasional Paper 134; ISBN 0 255 36555 1
£10.00

Towards a Liberal Utopia?
Edited by Philip Booth
Hobart Paperback 32; ISBN 0 255 36563 2
£15.00

The Way Out of the Pensions Quagmire
Philip Booth & Deborah Cooper
Research Monograph 60; ISBN 0 255 36517 9
£12.50

Black Wednesday
A Re-examination of Britain's Experience in the Exchange Rate Mechanism
Alan Budd
Occasional Paper 135; ISBN 0 255 36566 7
£7.50

Crime: Economic Incentives and Social Networks
Paul Ormerod
Hobart Paper 151; ISBN 0 255 36554 3
£10.00

The Road to Serfdom *with* The Intellectuals and Socialism
Friedrich A. Hayek
Occasional Paper 136; ISBN 0 255 36576 4
£10.00

Money and Asset Prices in Boom and Bust
Tim Congdon
Hobart Paper 152; ISBN 0 255 36570 5
£10.00

The Dangers of Bus Re-regulation
and Other Perspectives on Markets in Transport
John Hibbs et al.
Occasional Paper 137; ISBN 0 255 36572 1
£10.00

The New Rural Economy
Change, Dynamism and Government Policy
Berkeley Hill et al.
Occasional Paper 138; ISBN 0 255 36546 2
£15.00

The Benefits of Tax Competition
Richard Teather
Hobart Paper 153; ISBN 0 255 36569 1
£12.50

Wheels of Fortune
Self-funding Infrastructure and the Free Market Case for a Land Tax
Fred Harrison
Hobart Paper 154; ISBN 0 255 36589 6
£12.50

Were 364 Economists All Wrong?
Edited by Philip Booth
Readings 60
ISBN-10: 0 255 36588 8; ISBN-13: 978 0 255 36588 8
£10.00

Europe After the 'No' Votes
Mapping a New Economic Path
Patrick A. Messerlin
Occasional Paper 139
ISBN-10: 0 255 36580 2; ISBN-13: 978 0 255 36580 2
£10.00

To order copies of currently available IEA papers, or to enquire about availability, please contact:

Gazelle
IEA orders
FREEPOST RLYS-EAHU-YSCZ
White Cross Mills
Hightown
Lancaster LA1 4XS

Tel: 01524 68765
Fax: 01524 63232
Email: sales@gazellebooks.co.uk

The IEA also offers a subscription service to its publications. For a single annual payment, currently £40.00 in the UK, you will receive every monograph the IEA publishes during the course of a year and discounts on our extensive back catalogue. For more information, please contact:

Adam Myers
Subscriptions
The Institute of Economic Affairs
2 Lord North Street
London SW1P 3LB

Tel: 020 7799 8920
Fax: 020 7799 2137
Website: www.iea.org.uk